Carey On...

Carey Masci

Published by Shore-Line Publications

Carey Masci, Author

2-Sisters Editing Service Liz Schormuller and sister Marge, Editor

Creative Publishing Book Design, Book Formatter

Front & Back Cover © by Carey Masci

All Photographs Copyright © by Carey Masci

ISBN-13: 978-0-578-92717-6

Printed in the United States of America

Dedication

Bishop Davis—He prophesied many years before I even started writing that I would write a book. He even asked if I would be a guest on his radio show. I declined the invitation, thinking not me on the radio and me writing a book, never! Since that prophecy, I have written three books and been on the radio numerous times.

and

Michael Petro—Editor, publisher, author of numerous books, Christian patriot, and friend. He edited and published both of my previous books. I will sorely miss his guidance, his knowledge, and his friendship. He made a difference not only in my life but in the lives of many others.

Table of Contents

Preface

OH, OH. Some serious stuff here! I wanted to shoehorn into this book something about covid and its effect on our loss of freedom but wasn't sure what to write. Then I found something I had written on my laptop a few years back that I had forgotten. I was going to use it somehow as an introduction in my third book. I had no clue at the time how fitting it would be. Here it is:

Unfettered!

Unfettered – life and travel. Not to be confused with tethered, which is the complete opposite. Since I brought up the word tether, does anyone remember tetherball? I think that was when people started to become fettered — a ball attached to a rope hanging on a pole. To us kids, it was fun. But to adults, at least my Mom, they warned us to be careful, the ball could wrap around your neck, and you will choke and die. I don't ever remember reading he was a good kid, but that terrible tetherball choked out his life way too early.

So we untethered the ball and instead attached it to our psyche and became tethered or fettered. What the heck are you talking about, Carey? Um, I don't have a clue where I was going. OH, wait, now I remember, my point is being and living unfettered. According to Websters dictionary, 1828 edition, it gives this definition:

UNFET'TERED,

1. Unchained; unshackled; freed from restraint.

2. adjective Not restrained.

I like that. Let me sum it up this way in one word – FREEDOM! And that's how I choose to live my life and how I like to travel – free to go and do as I please.

Everywhere you go, no matter where you are, orders are barked, either at work or while watching TV where there is a constant bombardment of ads and the same with the PC and radio. So why do people choose to strap themselves in a car and listen to some computer-generated voice dictating directions? As I like to tell people, get lost and go find yourself. But you will never do so with some AI telling you where to go.

Sadly, however, today it has gone beyond AI dictating to you. Because of covid, whether real or contrived, our society in America, our American way of life are becoming more rule-oriented and restrictive. Our government has brainwashed people into accepting the loss of freedom because of fear of a virus you may or may never get. Daily more laws are passed. God and our God-given rights are being erased. Socialism and control are slowly being accepted by many. The masses are being – fettered.

I hope reading this book you will be encouraged to get out and experience all that life has to offer and fight to maintain your God-given freedoms. But if America does fall, I hope this book will stand as a testament to how free it was and give a glimpse into the great American road trip and life prior to covid and socialism.

Now let's have fun and go on a joy ride!

Note: Many of these stories occurred prior to the covid years, some places mentioned may have closed their doors.

Introduction

Hey Gang,

Thank you for joining me on another journey. For those who read my first two books, welcome back, and to those who are new to my writings, don't fasten that seat belt because these are freestyling adventures, unplanned fun, and unexpected "what now" stories.

As in the previous books, you may want to grab a highlighter to highlight the interesting places mentioned and visit them for yourself. And since this book expands beyond the road with stories closer to home and life, you may still want to use the highlighter to mark off things you shouldn't do. Just read on. You will understand.

Life Has Many Doors

Pastor Jim Porotosky once told me life has many doors. This was in reference to a rough spot I hit. Thinking it was over, I wondered now what?

We all go through this panic when something doesn't go right. Well, I realized life does indeed have many doors. One door may close, but others will open. And I got to thinking not only circumstances but also people, can be those doors. Anytime you meet someone, that encounter could enrich your life. It could lead you to a door that would never have been opened or challenge your thinking into seeing things differently.

I know that's a bit deep for a book that's lighthearted and fun in nature, but that's how the pen flowed. Besides, that thought is a good segue into how I came up with this book's title and the underlying theme of meeting people and unexpected happenings.

Name Game

My third book's original title was "Life is a Road Trip," but a search found that title was used many times. I like to be original, so it was time to hit refresh.

Everything I came up with or suggestions by others did not flow or sound right. On a Sunday drive, Cynthia, Donna, Ruth, and I were tossing ideas around. I wanted to use Carey on somehow in the title. Donna suggested travel light and Carey on. I said Nah, and almost immediately, Cynthia said, "Life, travel life!" That's it! Travel Life 'n" Carey On…

I worked on that title but wasn't completely convinced yet until I ran it past Tricia of Web Worx. She wrote,

"I love the play on words. I like that the same type of theme is carried through each cover."

I thought about what she said, and then it hit me what she meant. I read all my books titles together at once, "Hey Gang! Ready to Go-Go?", "Cruising Across America!", "Travel Life 'n' Carey On", hmmm.

Then I read them as a sentence:

Hey Gang, ready to go-go cruising across America, travel life, 'n' Carey on. It all came together. A door was opened.

I never envisioned writing one book, let alone three, and then having all the titles work together like that. I mean, how can you explain such a thing?

Furthermore, I love words and phrases that have double meanings. And that is called a – all together, ready – homonym, yes homonym.

Anyway, travel life can mean a few different things, as does Carey on. I don't think I have to explain further, do I?

So I had the content of my book, I had the title but then suddenly Michael Petro, my publisher/editor/proofreader/friend whom I mention in my dedication passed on. Now what do I do?

The Replacement

Skipping ahead, not literally, but if you want to skip, you can. Elliot calls and asks if I would like to meet him and his friend Liz at a restaurant. Earlier I had agreed to, but it was a long day. Eliot calls again and says, "Where are you, we're waiting." I reluctantly go.

Eliot introduces me to his friend Liz and tells her Carey's an author. What a perfect opportunity to promote my writings. I hand Liz my book, and immediately she says, wait, I have seen this before, but where. Not able to make the connection, we resume our conversation. Liz then tells us a story of working in the historical building at the Lake County Fair.

AHA! It came to us at the same time. We had previously met at the fair. Liz bought a copy of my book. Her friend borrowed it, so she never got the chance to read it.

I then find out Liz was a teacher. A teacher – whoa! So I asked her would you be interested in editing the book I'm writing. Without hesitation, she said, "YES!"

And just like that, a door was opened. I found my new editor/proofreader from an invite for coffee that I wasn't going to attend. Now isn't that neat!

My Third Book, Wow, a Third Book!

I love reading and writing; I could live in a book store though I don't know what my shelf life would be. And I feel my life has enough twists, turns, unexpected and unexplainable events that it makes for interesting storytelling. I make none of these stories up. They are all true.

On top of that writing to me is not only a hobby and passion but also rewarding. I enjoy conversing with people, especially ones who have read my books. Their response is always very positive, encouraging, and triggers stories of their own.

One of the best endorsements came from a client/friend who lives in a condo at the Park Building in downtown Cleveland.

This was written right after a fire in the mid-rise. Jesse wrote, "Carey you won't believe this, but we had to throw out everything, but as my wife was cleaning, she said HEY JESS LOOK! It was your book, Cruising Across America, I just ordered, it survived!"

Amazing! Besides being a great read, and an even better fly swatter and or doorstop, "Cruising Across America" will survive a fire. Um, I don't suggest you try setting your house on fire to see if this is true, thought I should put this disclaimer just in case someone was thinking of trying it. I hope you will find this third book, "Travel Life 'n" Carey On", lives up to the same billing.

Road Trips, Life and Laughs

As my Dad would say, and he'd say it quite often, live and learn. Most of the time, he said it while laughing. That was one of Dads great qualities, the ability to enjoy life and laugh at his blunders.

I thank him for passing that laughter on to me. Because of Dad always joking around, I also have learned to laugh at my own stupidity. Honestly, if you can't laugh at yourself, then who can you laugh at? Besides, life is too serious not to laugh – right?

In this third book, you'll find basically the same theme of road trips and travel being carried over from my previous works but expanded to include stories of my past and events that happened closer to home and not in any way travel-related. Though these events did make me want to hurry up, pack and get out of town real fast, but of course, while laughing!

Writing all that I have to ask, are you ready for twists, road trips, and the unexplained? If you are, I am ready to take off.

So jump aboard and let's

"Travel Life 'n" Carey On..."

Traveling through Arizona, I stopped at an Indian reservation. They wouldn't let me in. They said I needed a reservation.

Chapter One

School Boot Camp

Since I am digging through my archives for some of these stories for book three, my mind wandered back to one early camping experience that was anything but delightful. In fact, I was traumatized and hated every minute of it. The camp outing I speak of was sixth-grade school camp.

The school I attended, Lincoln Elementary, had an odd number of classes going to camp. Unfortunately, the odd numbered class was the one I was in. For this reason we had to go with another school, Mapledale.

Mapledale was still in Wickliffe, but when you are a child, the other side of a small city might as well be in another state. And since my class was outnumbered, the rivalry at camp was brutal. We were second-rate students even though Lincoln was the bigger school. It immediately started off badly. I remember a student whose nickname was Peanut, a name applied to him by his peers. I thought I would introduce myself, so I called him Peanut only to face the wrath of "What did you call me?" with his group of friends on standby ready to pummel me.

But the most unpleasant memory was the restrooms that smelled worse than an uncleaned dog kennel on a hot summer day. They were barracks-style pit toilets with more than one hole. I will skip over the rest of the details and instead write about bad memory number two – the food.

Oh yes, the food, oh my, the food. It was blah at best, but the worst meal was the spaghetti which was just plain awful. Especially being of Italian descent, to me it tasted worse than the toilets smelled. The spaghetti was so bad only a few of the students touched it. Most went without supper the day it was served. And I am not kidding when I say this; they kept serving it to us. The following day for supper, still no one ate it, and then there it was again. It was brought out to us for breakfast. What a cruel and unusual punishment!

Trouble was never far off for Lincoln or, well, um, me. One night our cabin secretly plotted against a fellow student whose name I will not mention. The plot was that we were going to pants him. Of course, I jumped up immediately and said, "I'll do it!". In the process, what happened? His PJ's ripped almost in half right before we locked him out of the cabin. There he was, pounding on the door screaming, let me in while trying to hold up his pajama bottom. Boy, oh boy, did I get blamed for being behind the whole scheme! I received a tongue lashing not only from the teachers, but from the boy's mother when she was called to bring another set of PJ's for him. The cabin got punished, and everyone blamed me. From there, it never got better.

The weather was cold and barely warmed up for the week. It even snowed a bit. It was one of the earliest snows ever. I didn't bring a winter coat, so mom and dad brought me one, and of course, being a kid, you know what ensued, relentless teasing. Aww, Carey is cold. Mommy and daddy brought him a coat!

Then we saw deer on a hike. Everyone was excited. The teacher said, "Shhh, don't move," but my over-exuberance of running to get closer spooked the deer, and off they went. Again everyone was mad at me; just another fond memory of the joy of school camp.

The next to last day of the five-day getaway was the awards ceremony for various events and for the cabins. The prize for the cleanest cabin was you could do as you pleased the last day. The messiest had to clean restrooms. 1 2 3 FLUSH! – 1 2 3 FLUSH! 1 2 3 FLUSH! over and over, it was chanted while the teachers read the list of the awards including which class had the cleanest cabin. Who came in last? Of course, Lincoln lost and received recognition for having the most unruly and unkempt cabin. And I being dumb and naive, bought into the whole thing, "NO WAY ARE THEY LOWERING ME INTO THE TOILET TO CLEAN IT OUT", which was the word being passed around. 1 2 3 FLUSH I was horrified that I would be literally lowered into the pit to bucket out the poop. I still hear it every so often when I see an old-fashioned pit toilet – 1 2 3 FLUSH!

Were there any good memories? There were a few like the first night there we had an assembly about Indians. No one could guess what made the sound in these small handheld drums except me – cherry pits. Everyone was amazed goof off Carey would know that, but then I fell asleep. Mr. Benigar, I believe it was him, thought I had passed out or something. I remember him shaking me and asking, "Hey, are you all right?"

A few friendships were made. I met Pat Frank and sat with him and his friends in the dining hall. Pat taught us how to "Burp the baby." What the heck is "Burp the baby?" He would shake up the little milk carton, barely open it, squeeze the sides, and bubbles of milk would come out. At that age, we were all impressed by this amazing act.

But the best good memory was winning an award for finding the most fossils, 23 to be exact. I still have the paper award honoring my accomplishment. Those were the bright moments that didn't even come close to outweighing the bad. It is a wonder that I like camping at all after that brutal experience.

Chapter Two

The Great Stoneboro Fair

Every summer should include a festival or two and a fair. If it doesn't, to me, it's just not complete.

This write up is when I attended The Great Stoneboro Fair – "Always on Labor Day" and hailed as "A Family Tradition For Over 150 Fairs!"

This is small-town America at its finest when everyone local gathers. The fair was organized way back in 1868 by the "Mercer County Agricultural and Manufacturing Society of Stoneboro." The trip to this fair was memorable not only for what it offered but because I got to wear a cup of coffee.

Stoneboro is a borough in Mercer County, Pennsylvania. I forgot how hilly Pennsylvania is. When I think of hills and mountains, I think of West Virginia or Tennessee, but the Keystone State sure has its share of up and down and twisty roads.

The parking lot is on a hill, and the fairgrounds are quite unique. It is separated by a high and low section accessible by two tunnels that you walk through. In between the high and low areas is the track for various events, such as the popular demolition derby.

It has not one but two demolition derbies, an adult and a kiddie. The adult derby was a blast. The crowd was really into it, but the lady I sat next to got a wee bit too animated. During the smash ups she punched her husband and then turned and pushed me. My coffee went for a ride, landing on me. And that is how I got to wear a cup of coffee. She apologized and said, "I get a little excited." I said "It's OK, but next time I sit next to you, I'm wearing a raincoat."

The hilly parking lot
Stoneboro Fair, Pennsylvania

One of the two tunnels connecting both sides of the fair
Stoneboro, Pennsylvania

As for the kiddie demolition derby at first, I thought it was dumb. It was actually pretty funny and entertaining watching the children drive their little pedal cars into each other.

The fair also had a slew of food vendors, rides, livestock, a wildlife exhibit that is quite impressive, and a huge antique tractor gathering which, even though I may be from a city suburb, I really enjoyed. There is far more to this fair than what I listed. But why should I ruin it for you? Go experience it yourself.

The admission to get in includes the whole shebang – rides and entertainment – so not a bad deal for some end-of-summer fun.

OH, one more thing. If you go during the day you've got to stay till nighttime. The night view from Gate 2 overlooking the midway is so spectacular it will bring out the little kid in you.

A colorful and exciting night view of the midway
Stoneboro Fair, Pennsylvania

Chapter Three

Day Escape to Cook Forest

For the most part, things went well on this three-day escape which was another quickly planned getaway. It was a quieter trip, a trip to unclutter the mind as the camp chaplain preached.

A week before Labor Day, I asked Nick, "Do you want to go camping"? We agreed on Cook Forest, once called the Black Forest, in Pennsylvania, somewhere that I have never visited. It was the right choice as our route drove us through areas that I have never seen.

In many of my travel log/stories, a weather report is included because it could make or break a trip. It plays a big part in making travel pleasant or miserable. It also makes the reader really experience the journey. For this trip, the weather was quite ideal Friday through early Sunday morning. It briefly stormed, dried up, and didn't rain again till we started driving home late afternoon on Labor Day. All days were hot and sunny, a perfect way to end the summer travel season.

The trip started off with a stop at a local gas station in Wickliffe to fill up, and that's when Nick walked back to the Go-Go Bus after paying and told me to look under it. His face told the story. I was chicken to look and kept asking what? Just look. So I did, and OH no, what's that leaking? Gas! Pulled it to the side of the station, crawled under, and found the culprit. The small hose from the gas filter to the gas pump was chewed? It seemed that way to me. Nick said, "Naww," and I said, "Yes, gnaw." I have a mice problem in my garage, and in the Go-Go Bus, I've seen them scamper. When I opened the engine cover, mouse poop was found on top of my engine and in the potato chip bowl left on the table. Didn't know mice like rubber hoses or BBQ chips. I am thankful the line ruptured close to home and not on the freeway. A quick repair and off we went

We were making OK time, but the Bus was running rough, so we stopped before Youngstown at Craig Woodruff's place. Craig rebuilds carbs. He gave my carb a few adjustments and said, have a nice trip. We took notes from him of places to see in Cooks Forest and headed back to Rt. 80.

We made it to Shippendale, the place I thought the male strippers came from, when I realized it's Shippenville and much later on, I realized it's Chippendale. Driving through town we saw a tiny grocery store, "Red & White", a real throwback. It had signs in front like the old Burma Shave, one after the other. The smoked pork chops sign was the one that got my attention. The store looked inviting outside and inside as well. It has wood floors with mounted heads of animals hanging on the wall. The shelves had essential groceries, some dry goods, produce, and in the back, the butcher counter, deli, and a small room where the smoking and making of jerky happens. The smell of the place was, oh my goodness, heavenly!

The owner's name is Dan Stiller. They asked if we wanted to try their bologna. I wish I would have. I noticed later their business card said, "Try our almost famous bologna & other smoked meats." After a few laughs, we left.

It's a good thing I didn't listen to Nick. He didn't want to stop. Not only because we found quality meat but because we were going in the wrong direction. Dan directed us to Rt. 66 and said head towards Leeper, and we did.

One more stop before the campground at another Red & White for pop which we forgot at the other Red & White. They are not related or a chain, according to the first one we stopped at.

A short distance from the campground entrance, we saw road flares and a patrol car with flashers going. A little bit further, there were more emergency vehicles, a tow truck, and someone directing traffic around an accident. This was a YouTube moment, if there ever was one. The emergency workers, paramedics, or whatever they were stopped look up and said, "Hey, neat vehicle!" "Oh my gosh, look at that!" I am sure the injured party involved in the wreck wasn't too thrilled to see the Go-Go Bus, though.

Preparing our meal
Cook Forest, Pennsylvania

Nick was excited as we set up camp. This was his first tent experience. He usually sleeps in the car. After supper, I took a nap. I wake up just about to exit the Bus when a Pennsylvania ranger's patrol car stops abruptly; two officers get out in a hurry with flashlights drawn. My mind raced. Was it the wood we took, the electric hot plate I am using, IRS coming to get me? I must have seemed scared because the one said to me, "Oh, you are not in trouble. We just wanted to see your vehicle." But they sure must have thought I was stoned. If you don't know me, it's this way after a nap or just waking… silence please, coffee and OK now you can talk. I forgot where I was and said, "You're from the NY police?" Duh! They enjoyed the brief tour of the Bus and took off.

It was the first time cops asked politely if they could look in my vehicle, and the first time I more than obliged. After they exited, Nick told me, "You weren't the only one scared." But that's for Nick to tell you why; that's his story, not mine.

Speaking of Nick, he did something I have never seen before. He brought along air freshener and was spraying around our campsite. I said, "That has to be the weirdest thing I've seen. Who sprays a campsite?" Nick replied, "That's weird? What about the things you do", and then he rattled off a list. Why was Nick spraying the campsite, and what was on his list about me? Well, once again, I have to repeat that's for Nick to tell you why, that's his story, not mine, so that's all I will say. Now let's continue.

Saturday morning arrived, and the park chaplain came by to invite us to the Sunday service in the park. We small talked a bit, then I mentioned the rangers that stopped last night to look at the Bus. The guy in the adjacent site heard us and came over. He said, "I'm a lawyer, and when I saw the rangers talking to you and looking inside your vehicle last night, I thought to myself, this guy needs a lawyer, but when they left, I stayed put, now I know what happened." How 'bout that! I was in good hands… oh, wait, that's an insurance commercial, never mind. It was time for some hiking.

15

The part of Cook Forest we stayed at is beautiful. The old-growth pines are of incredible height. The smell of pine is so aromatic. There are plenty of trails from easy to difficult but no real breathtaking vistas or scenery. One scenic overlook though, was Seneca Point, and the view from the fire tower we climbed was also picturesque. Both of these are across from Ridge Campground, where we stayed.

The fire tower seemed to sway. It was crazy. The tower was taken out of service years ago, and the reason for that shows. The height is listed at 80 feet, and the sign said it looks over the 130-foot tall pines. How is this possible? I don't know. If you find out, let me know. A mother and her young daughter started to climb up. The lady chickened out, so the husband took the daughter and their toddler son. She told us I am a very protective mother, but I can't look. I thought to myself neither one would win the parent of the year award. The steps are open and so easy for a kid to slip through. They were from Eastlake, which is a city over from where I live. Maybe that has something to do with it.

The trail we hiked was the Longfellow Trail, only 1.2 miles in length. Some of the white pines on this trail are over 400 years old and are the tallest in the Northeastern US at 150 feet. One tree they measured is 183 feet.

Sunday morning at 5:00 a.m. I awoke from a bizarre dream. A storm was approaching that turned into a tornado. At the base of this twirling funnel cloud were Batman & Robin with their arms crossed, shielding me. They were HUGE. I ran inside to tell my family, and they responded, this is no storm but a tornado, hide. I was awoken from this dream by a loud CRACK and BOOM. I looked out the window, startled. It had woke Nick also, and he said calmly as only Nick could, "Yes Carey, it's a thunderstorm." Now don't go writing to me saying my guardian angels must be superheroes. It was only a dream… or was it?

Nick and I thought we were in for a bad storm, so I grabbed the large tarp I brought for him to throw over his tent for added protection. But it quickly passed through with just a quick downburst. I fell asleep for a few more hours and woke about 8:30 a.m. just in time for church service.

A quick bowl of cereal and two cups of coffee, and we were off to the amphitheater of the park for Sunday service. I stopped at the trailer of the park host, greeted them good morning, introduced myself, and then asked would you happen to have a chair I could borrow for church? I was planning to sit on the grass, but because of the rain earlier that isn't possible. They were more than happy to lend a chair. Nick didn't feel like asking, so we left with only a chair for me.

Have any of you ever attended church in a park or outdoors? It's really something special and even more so when it's held early morning at a campground in a national forest.

The grass was damp, the sun was out, temps were warming, and behind the Park Chaplain was a backdrop of tall trees and greenery, a gorgeous setting for a sermon. It was a small gathering of about ten.

The park chaplain had the perfect demeanor for an outdoor pastor. He dresses in casual clothing with a wooden cross around his neck that a camper made for him, a warm smile that is welcoming and very down to earth. He preached on uncluttering your mind. He went on to say how he used to get upset that some in the campground were not attending service that he knew were good Christians. And then he thought to himself, maybe these people are so caught up with their home church activities, being a deacon or asked to do so much at church that this was their chance just to take a break, a time to unclutter their mind. The meaning of the sermon was how busy we all are that we need to relax, quit being in such a hurry, take time to hear God. It was a short sermon, but he got his message across of uncluttering the mind.

We went back to the park host and, before I handed the chair back, said "The sermon was great and not only that I had the best seat in the park, thank you." The husband-wife team just laughed and wished us a good day.

Nick and I got back to the Go-Go Bus to wrap things up but were slightly delayed by one of the park workers. He came over and politely asked do you mind if I take some photos of your vehicle? Well, gee, of course not. Across from our lot was someone waiting to pull in. He saw what was going on with the photo op and said, don't worry, take your time.

We got the Bus loaded and then don't ask me what happened to Nick, but suddenly his mind became anxious and cluttered. We are going home now, right? Huh, home? No way, we are in Pennsylvania, it's Sunday during a holiday weekend, and the last weekend of the vacation season, there is NO WAY I am heading straight back home. It started an unpleasant exchange of words and nerves.

I blew it off, but before I did, I said to Hurry Up Nick, "YOU DID NOT LISTEN TO THE SERMON, DID YOU? WELL, I AM GOING TO UNCLUTTER MY MIND AND ENJOY MYSELF." And that's what I did.

From Cook Forest, we went to the Clear Creek area not too far from the campground we stayed, about a 20-minute drive if that. The Clear Creek campground is far more scenic. Another place I have to come back to. We hiked another short trail inside this park, but antsy Nick wanted to get, and the clouds that moved in wanted to go, and they did, so Nick got his wish, and we went. And that concluded the three-day trip that at least uncluttered my mind.

I drove my friend Gary who was heading to Indiana to the train station. He is more reserved, quieter and at times, likes to be left alone and I was in one of my off-the-wall talkative moods.

Gary and I were standing waiting for the train when a man walked by. Of course I struck up a conversation with him. He was polite and a nice person, but he sure was a chatterbox. In a short span I knew about his daughter, his ex, the time he had to go to court for mortgage fraud for working with someone who was shady, and 20 other different things.

I introduced him to Gary. He turned around and started up with Gary. Gary slowly backed away, found a seat, and left me there with Mr. Filibuster. I didn't care, as it was an opportune time to ask the guy if he could do me a favor and look out for my friend, whatever you do please keep checking on Gary and talk to him all you can. He doesn't like trains or being alone, he is a little nervous; please I would appreciate this.

Chapter Four

Scary

I am reaching far back with this faded photograph of a trip with Julie to visit Ed Coster in Moundsville, West Virginia.

This trip actually wasn't one of the better adventures I have ever taken. But it did have a few panic moments that, when I recall them, they still haunt me, and that grip of fear grabs hold memomentarily.

Tygart Dam
West Virginia

I will skip over and won't mention – the shooting lesson Julie passed, and I flunked – the suffocating tropic-like heat sleeping in the van with the windows having to be up because of a relentless rain, the picturesque morning with fog lazily lifting as I stood in amazement of the view atop a bridge overlooking the Tygart Dam while Julie refused to stir from her slumber. Nope, I'm not going to write about those memories at all but will write about the two horrific moments that linger vividly in the recesses of my mind.

We were in Ohio traveling on I-77 south heading to West Virginia when a rest break was summoned. Drink, snack, and relief, not necessarily in that order, but you know what I mean. I still remember the exact exit; it was the Byesville exit.

Now keep in mind that I am going back to the vault for this story when cell phones were few and only for the rich. As I approached the exit, the local AM station we were listening to, broke with an alert about an escapee from a state mental hospital who was charged with rape. The announcer warned if traveling be cautious and do not pick up hitchhikers.

We got and did what we stopped for and started back towards the entrance of I-77 when sure enough, there was a hitchhiker standing on the side of the road. What the hey, Carey knows no stranger plus it would be spooky fun, maybe he is the man – OOO. "HEY, ya need a ride?" Julie was not too keen. Actually, she was upset because of what we just heard minutes earlier. He jumps in. I have no recollection of his name, can't really recall his looks other than he was palish white, sort of a short bowl-cut uncombed brown hair, stature short, and quietly odd. He didn't speak much, but he was heading to West Virginia also, Wheeling to be exact, which is the way to Moundsville.

Not much was said on the 50 miles or so ride there. We drive to his house. We asked to use the bathroom. On the way out of his house, I went to shake his hand. As he reached for mine, his sleeve went up and on his wrist was a hospital name tag bracelet. It spooked us badly. We quickly zoomed out of there. Was it him? Was it?

Scary Part 2

Now, this was only scary for me. I told Julie about it immediately after I saved myself from dying. Everyone knows Carey is never far from joking, so did she take me seriously? I don't know.

If you kept up with my travels, you know Carey might lack a shower but never lacks finding a way to keep clean. I had to find a beach to freshen up, which is quite an oft-occurring scene in my books.

Driving through Tygart State Park, there was a beach. I pulled into the short parking lot. I got out and what greeted me was a padlocked, tall, chain-linked fence with a tin sign hanging that read BEACH CLOSED.

I still remember the setting, the lot, trees/woods on both sides of the small old-style brick bathhouse, a small sandy beach. It was summer, quiet, very clean looking, so it didn't make sense why the beach was closed.

The chain was not much of a deterrent as I spread the gates apart and squeezed myself through. As I said, the sandy beach was tiny, then there was flat rock with shallow water that barely went above my feet, and maybe ten to fifteen-foot distance to the water's edge.

Once past the gate with the towel swung over my shoulder, I carefreely walked through the sand and onto the whoops, slippery flat rocks. Bam, I fell on my back and was sliding towards the abyss. I mean ABYSS.

I remember sliding closer and closer to the edge where it dropped straight down, quarry-like. Maybe this was the beach before the river was dammed and made into a lake? Maybe that's why it was closed? The water in these parts is clear, and let me tell you, I saw nothing. I still remember the panic. I tried gripping the rocks, but there was nothing to grab hold of to save me from sliding in. I am not much of a swimmer, and even if I was, how could I get out?

So what saved me? When I got scared, I stiffened like a board. As I was slipping, I coolly calmed down and relaxed and somehow crawled back up towards the beach. Julie was just approaching. I told her what just happened and said, "Let's just get out of here."

I am very serious. I was inches, I mean inches from drowning, and who knows when I would have been dredged up. I learned my lesson, closed beach means closed beach. Never again!

Well... there was one other time with Walt at Greenbo Lake in Kentucky that had a closed sign, but that's another story for another book.

Chapter Five

Tennessee and Back
A Hey Gang Play-by-Play as it Happened
No Commercials, Uninterrupted in All its
Glory, Nothing Left Out

I did not have time to write things as they happened, so I will play catch up. However, I did manage to make notes, will report from them and my recollection. I dubbed this trip the throwback trip. Just about everything we did or saw had a connection to the past. The Go-Go Bus is a '69 and just driving in it gives you a feel of yesterday. The convention I attended had to do with restoring the nation to the way it was years ago, we saw Elvis's house, the MLK memorial, the old hotel we stayed in, Cave City, Lincoln's birthplace, the junk antique shops; it was just an awesome flashback trip.

Currently, I am at Look Out Restaurant writing as Ruth, Dan, and Paul pack, and I finish my morning breakfast of coffee and orange juice. That should get me going in more ways than one.

The purpose of this trip was to attend the Constitution Party Convention held in Memphis. When I agreed to attend it at the state convention last fall, my hopes were my wallet would be filled and the cost of gas stabilized to somewhat affordable levels. Well, my wallet is only half full, and gas has risen, so I was very hesitant about going to Memphis. State Chairman Don emailed me and said Dan from Columbus needs a ride, maybe you could carpool it. The gas to Tennessee and back in the Go-Go Bus would be about $450, so even with Dan, things would be tight, but the Bus has everything I need.

Part 2

Lately, I'm not sure what had gotten into me because I have been running on time. Ruth and I had everything packed and just about ready when Paul pulled into my drive at 9:30 a.m. We even arrived on time at 1:00 p.m. to pick up Dan in Columbus, but before hitting the road, there was a slight problem with the Go-Go Bus which always seems to happen.

Rewinding to the beginning, we stopped at the corner market by my house for last-minute snacks. We came out, and the Bus didn't start. I played with the wires and nothing. While I'm under the dash, a car stops right in front. I look up briefly, not paying too much attention because someone is always coming up to it, so at first, I didn't recognize him. But I did a double-take and notice it's my brother Craig.

He got out and asks, "What's up"? He happened to be on vacation and was just coming from the veterinarian down the street. What timing, that he should pass at that exact time and had jumper cables. He gave the Bus a jump. It started instantly. I told Paul "As long as we get to Memphis, I don't care what happens once there." Paul said, "Well, you won't believe this, but I just prayed seconds before your brother stopped."

All the way to Memphis and back, the entire trip, the Bus ran fine, never another glitch with the starting or charging.

Part 3

My goal was to arrive in Memphis no later than 11:00 p.m. We passed Cincinnati right on schedule, and I started thinking I can do this, but about 60 miles or so from Louisville, traffic just stopped, then crawled. We asked several truckers what was up. They had no clue, but two women in a car

25

next to us did. They told us this backup is for miles, follow us, we are exiting at the next exit and taking the old route. So that's what I did, and it cost me at least an hour and a half, maybe more.

What happened was I decided to forget the old route the women suggested but found an alternative way back to the freeway – Rt. 142 to Rt. 55, which is a twisty country road back to the highway Rt. 71. Things went smoothly for a while until Rt. 55. Traffic was stopped again, this time for an extra-wide semi pulling a house. Every so often, it would pull over and let oncoming traffic through. This was worse than the mess on the highway. That's how we lost time and were thrown off our pace.

I've had the Go-Go Bus for over 20 years, and I still have fun with it. At a gas station somewhere in Kentucky, four cackling, silly women came up to me asking, what is this, who are you with? The next thing I know, they were sitting in the Go-Go Bus taking photos of each other. They were from Indiana heading to Orleans. If you're out there, Hoosier Girls, hope you are well and still smilin' and laughin'.

Part 4

Our arrival time of 2:45 a.m. at the hotel in Memphis wasn't bad, considering everything. There was the stop to pick up Dan in Columbus, the traffic mess, the hard rain we ran into, plus exiting the freeway every 200 miles to refuel. So 745 miles in a slow-moving house-car in 15 hours and 45 minutes ain't bad. Dan and Paul shared a room. Ruth and I took the Bus and parked far back in the hotel parking lot.

The hotel lacked any frills; it was strictly for business and conventions. It did have one unexpected surprise in Dan and Paul's room. I went in first with Dan's bag. While he was being wheeled in, he asked loudly does this room have any bedbugs. The porter helping with his wheelchair was about to answer, when I said, "No, but they do have large animals!" There was a cockroach so big it looked like an animal. The porter said, "Oh, it's a water bug." He grabbed toilet paper, stood on a chair, and went to squash it but missed. The bug fell, and the porter did a lively dance making sure the thing wasn't on him. It took two stomps to kill it. It was a nice welcome; after that, though, no other bugs were found.

I always sleep well in the Go-Go Bus, probably better than at home. It's that comfy. I was in a sound sleep when I heard these LOUD bangs, just a horrible sounding bad noise. I turned on my sleep/sound machine, started to fall asleep, and there it was again. It happened a few times. Not sure if it was thunder, sonic booms, gunfire; who knows. Why do I always hear bangs and booms on my trips?

Part 5

Morning came, and I was a bit late for the start of the Constitution Party Convention. The convention was not your typical political convention. It was laid back. Those in attendance were more for lack of better words, everyday voters who decided to get involved. I am sure there were a few lawyers and elected officials who decided to leave the establishment parties, but that's OK; you do need their knowledge and experience.

The national chairman of the party is Frank Fluckiger. His demeanor was quiet, soft-spoken, and very likable. Far different from other political leaders I have met, Frank seemed real and sincere. He had time for joking and nonpolitical talk. I really liked him.

There was little discussion about defeating the opposing party, unlike Republican meetings, where it's all about downing and defeating

27

the Democrats at any cost, all the while abandoning party platform and principles to do it. A few of the topics our conversation and dialog centered around were: getting to know other party members from different states, how to organize the party, networking ideas, how to dispel the myth that a third-party candidate can't win, furthering the Constitution Party for our ultimate goal of winning elections to restore our nation, our liberties and our freedom.

When day one ended, I asked someone at the convention, who lives in Memphis what there was to see. She suggested a drive through an area downtown by the river, but advised, don't get out and walk around like I wanted. She said it wasn't a safe area. Ruth, Paul, and I took a vote and instead chose to drive to Graceland, even though it wouldn't be open.

We followed the travel brochure to Graceland, but somehow got lost. I asked a woman at a gas station for directions. She gave them, left the gas station, turned around, came back, and said, just follow me, I'll take you there. Now that's southern hospitality at its finest.

Driving towards Graceland, you see this mirage-like structure with a stone fence around it. The fence is high enough that viewing the mansion is difficult. Graffiti and signatures cover the stone barrier and make it look almost ghetto-like. On TV it is always shown in a tight shot, so it appears much different from seeing it in person.

I just couldn't believe where Graceland was located. What a sad surprise. It is shoehorned between junk stores and strip mall after strip mall. I was as disappointed as when I saw the Alamo in Texas. The Alamo is also surrounded by stores and tacky tourist shops. PLEASE don't think I am comparing the Alamo to Graceland, only comparing their placement.

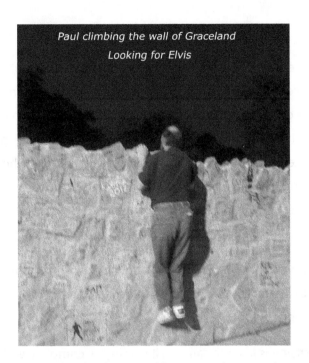
Paul climbing the wall of Graceland
Looking for Elvis

I pictured Graceland to be more like a sprawling southern plantation with nothing around or in an upscale community. Maybe years ago, when it was built, the area was like that. I wondered if Elvis were alive today, would his neighborhood have declined as it has, or if he would have fled and moved elsewhere.

Across the street was an Elvis-themed gift shop and diner plus both of his airplanes, which you could also tour. Next door, there are tacky tourist shops touting all things Elvis.

It was just really weird seeing it, again much different from what I expected. All the idol worship people give this man, you would think leading up to Graceland, the streets would be paved of gold, or at least gold records.

I was all shook up…

Part 6

From the King of Rock & Roll to another more important King. After leaving Graceland, we stopped at a little place for wings and fries. We took the food to go. My inner compass just about got us back to downtown Memphis when a light went on, and I said, "Hey, didn't MLK get shot in Memphis? Let's go find the hotel." We asked a few people who knew the place and the general direction, but when we got close, we had to ask again. A third time we asked, and a man said, "Follow me, I will take you there"; again, another example of Southern hospitality.

I had no clue that the motel was now a civil rights museum and a memorial to Martin Luther King Jr. It was eerie and made more so because of the late hour we saw it.

The outside is just the same as it was in '68, complete with cars that were the correct model year when the assassination took place and are parked exactly as they were on that fateful day.

It was a very somber place, but the backdrop of noise from people partying at the bars showed the memorial little respect. It made me reflect that this man gave his life to the struggle of bettering African Americans and really all Americans, from prejudice, but people abuse it and don't care about how they talk, dress, or act at a place honoring him. What would MLK think of what is going on today?

MLK had a dream, and in some respects, part of that dream never became a reality: and not because of what he did, but because people today refuse to do the right thing.

My thoughts on Memphis is it's an interesting city. Parts are quite seedy-looking, but the city did have life and plenty of history. I found it quite amusing that the cable car tracks are in the middle of the road, literally. Not sure how traffic moves when the cable car runs. The cable cars are restored from an earlier era.

It was time to retire; day two of the Constitution Party Convention would start early. Hopefully, better road tales lay ahead.

Part 7

Seeing the MLK site haunted my thoughts, though I slept quite well. As usual, I woke late and missed part of the lectures at the convention. The one topic I was really sorry I missed was the topic on the effects of illegal aliens on our nation. Other topics were the danger of a Constitutional Convention (ConCon), common core, social issues for dummies, and the importance of issues in political campaigns.

It was great to be in a room with people from different walks of life, states, and religions but who agreed with helping this nation and stopping the Federal Government from encroaching into our personal freedom and liberties.

The Constitution Party Preamble reads:

We the members of the Constitution Party gratefully acknowledge the blessing of the Lord God as Creator, Preserver, and Ruler of the Universe and of this Federal Republic. We hereby appeal to Him for aid, comfort, guidance, and the protection of His Divine Providence.

I met Daniel from Georgia, a logger from Colorado, a preacher from Tennessee; maybe I shouldn't list anymore because I know I am leaving many out.

The two-day convention went way too fast. I hated to leave so quickly, but we had a long haul ahead of us, so short goodbyes were said; then we headed out to find our hotel in Park City, Kentucky.

Time was approaching 9:00 p.m. , so with a raise of hands, we voted to stop off in Nashville to eat. What a bad vote that was. From the little we saw, Nashville is no longer a country city. It is far different from years back when I was there as a kid on a family vacation and again about 20 or so years ago.

Saturday night was crazy busy. We thought we could find a nice country restaurant or something different than what we have at home, but all we ran into were chain restaurants. We stopped at a little independent diner, but it was just closing. My temp gauge on the Bus started rising, so we ventured to the outskirts of the city, but still nothing. Finally, we found a Mexican restaurant and ate there. The food was decent, but our waitress understood very little English.

What happened to ham, grits, greens, and taters?

Part 8

After our run-around Nashville episode, the drive up to Park City was smooth. We drove through Bowling Green and probably could have saved time and found a better meal if we had eaten there.

Park City is actually a small town and a small town that time had forgotten. Near the freeway exit, a corporate dollar store had sprouted. Little else in the town from the old days had survived; like so many other towns in America.

Getting off the freeway, we guessed at the right way to go, but that dead-ended into 31-W, not to be confused with 31-E. I never did figure out how you could be on 31-W and head east or west or north, and on 31-E, you could go north and south; anyway on 31-W we went the wrong way. Not far from the exit was an old, flat, one-story motel that had a car jacked up with the motel room table lamps underneath. Someone at 1:00 a.m. was working on their car. I decided to pull in and ask for directions.

Well, it hit me and hit me hard. I had a laugh time. Anyone that knows me really well knows that a laugh time can come on suddenly without notice. I just sized up the situation of this site – old motel, car jacked up, tools sprawled all around, table lamps plugged in, with a man working on his car. What were his neighbors thinking, or if it was still a motel, the other guests? It occurred to me, this must be my twin because I do the same thing, and I started to laugh and laugh.

The man crawled out from under his car to talk to us, but it was no use. No matter what he said, a loud BAH HA HA came out. He had to think I was doped up. It was bad. Dan listened as best as he could. I quickly pulled out with tears in my eyes and vague directions.

Laughing is always good before a fright – time to find Park Mammoth Resort.

Part 9

Leaving the few lights in town for nothing but darkness we quickly went from laughing, to nervously saying, is this where we will be staying?

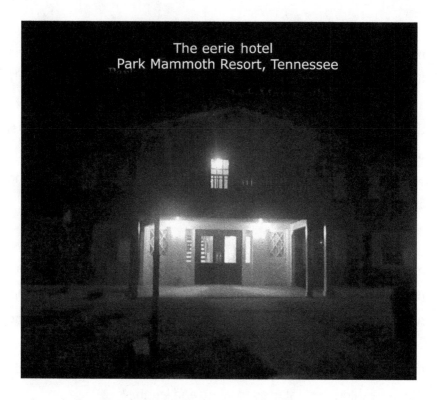

The eerie hotel
Park Mammoth Resort, Tennessee

What made the motel even eerier was the steep incline leading to it. Once you get to the top, you just about enter the parking lot, and there it was – dark and gloomy.

The best way to describe Park Mammoth Resort is a coelacanth, a real throwback, and I mean, a real throwback to years ago. It's only two stories high but spread out in a western ranch fashion, dark brown siding with dim bulbs lighting it.

The overhang where you parked under to enter the lobby was also poorly lit. Once you entered, it didn't get much brighter. The lobby, sign-in desk, and dining area were as dark as the outside. It looks considerably older than the year it was built – 1964. I learned why it looked so ancient. They built it to look rustic and old; so you add the old look they wanted, plus 50 years of use with no improvements makes the place look really spooky old. Very little has been updated, if anything. I was told at one time this was the resort at which to stay. The golf course, caves on the property, shooting range, swimming pool, a little train circling the hotel, and, if I heard correctly, it sits on 2,000 acres, all made it the place to vacation. I believe the winery and wine tasting room were recently added; they are in the slow process of updating, so you better visit soon if you are into time-warps.

The women at the front desk were quite friendly. They handed us our room keys and explained the rooms had air-conditioning but it was only turned on during certain months, so if we get hot, they could give us a fan. And yes, I wrote – a room key – no cards in this place. I loved it.

I walked the place before retiring for the night. The halls were sparse, and by the entrances, old yellowed framed photos hung on the wall. The one that startled me was the one with the hand. It seemed as if, one time, their honored guest, Thing, from the Addams Family, stayed or maybe this was their place. I walked out on one balcony that had a small table, and on top were numerous small candles arranged in a circle. Yikes! What ritual went on here?

What about that time warp smell? Well, yes, it had that too. In our house, we call that smell moofa, an Italian word and spelled as we say it. You know that damp smell found in an old musty, basement or cellar filled with old things? Well, that's the smell. In today's sanitized world of man-made products, even smells have changed, but not in this place. The resort's smell reminded me of yesterday, my grandma's house. After a while, that smell actually became like an old friend returning and brought back memories. I started to miss it when I left. Say it one more time with me – MOOFA.

Thing from the Addams Family?
Park Mammoth Resort, Tennessee

Part 10

Sunday, I awoke and turned on my pocket transistor AM/FM radio to an AM station playing terrific songs of yesterday, not just top 40 oldies, but forgotten oldies at least in the Cleveland area they are. And yes, I still carry a pocket transistor radio. I feel it is a must to have one for weather alerts when traveling; plus I just like it, no-frills, just 2 watts of awesome treble sound.

The other sound we woke to was the sound of gunshots. At first, I thought someone was hunting, maybe a little too close to the resort, or worse, but that's when I remembered on the grounds was a shooting range, thank goodness. Nothing like peace and quiet, right? That reminded me that when I made the reservations; the lady told me they have a golf course and a shooting range. I told her I don't do either, but if I do get a hole in one, it may be because I misfired a gun and not because I was good on the golf course.

We met Dan and Paul for breakfast at the restaurant inside the hotel called Look Out Restaurant. I asked the waitress if the name Look Out was because of the lookout from the dining area or because the food is so bad you need to look out? She laughed, but in reality, I think it was named for both reasons. The scenery is terrific and added to the rustic old décor of the restaurant, and the food, well it was average at best, so if you're wanting a good meal, look out!

Ruth looking out the window of the Look Out Restaurant

We decided on finding a church before our next adventure of touring the caves. One of the things I love doing when traveling is attending local churches. I love to experience how others worship and conduct their service, plus it really gives you a feel for the area you are visiting. Paul asked our waitress, whose dad just happenened to be a pastor. She gave us directions to Rocky Hill Baptist Church.

Part 11

Rocky Hill Baptist church wasn't too far from our hotel but definitely out in the country. Sunday service had already started when we arrived. We entered and took our seats as quietly as possible. The preacher was in the middle of preaching up a storm. His style was a throwback to the tent revivals of years past, loud, boisterous, and very animated.

The church itself was also reminiscent of years past, even though it was recently built. The pews were wooden, a piano was the only instrument, and they still used hymn books, which to me is the only way to sing hymns.

We enjoyed the service, but what we found strange was the unorthodox manner in which someone joins their congregation. A woman stood up and gave a lengthy testimony about her struggles and how she had drifted. She went on for some time about how she had repented and will stay committed to God. Then she said "I want to become a member of this church." The pastor said "OK, let's take a vote." But before he said anything further, someone else spoke up and verbally gave his support to the lady, saying I feel she's sincere. The pastor then said "Alright, let's take a vote. All in favor, say aye." The small congregation gave a loud "Aye." "Anyone against?" It was silent, so her membership was approved right there.

Part 12

Church ended, and everyone left rather quickly. There was time for introductions and handshakes, and thanks for attending our church, but it was brief. I spoke with the pastor outside, and maybe this is too obvious to print, but he was very alarmed by what is happening in this country, and especially what is coming out of Washington, D. C. Even this far out in the middle of nowhere, people are paying attention.

I asked the pastor's wife what there was to see in the way of parks, scenic lookouts, or whatever? She recommended heading to Mammoth Cave National Park. Besides the caves, it's an excellent park system with lots of acres. I said, "Perfect, we were thinking of going there anyway to see the caves, but what about bears? Are there any bears around here? Ruth wants to pet a bear." The lady was a bit alarmed and replied, "Well, there may be some bears around here, but you don't want to try and pet them, that's dangerous." Ruth remarked later, "I don't know what's dumber, someone asking if there are bears we can pet or someone answering that question?"

We returned to the hotel to change our clothes and to check on Dan. He was alright and gave us his blessings to have a good time caving while he stayed put inside the hotel.

On our way to Mammoth Caves Park, we stopped at yet another throwback, Big Mikes Rock Shop, billed as Kentucky's largest gift shop. There were signs leading up to Big Mikes with huge arrows pointing the way. Their signs had intrigue and mystery written all over them; Mystery House – Come see Big Mo a one of a kind attraction in the world – Kentucky's largest gift shop – You'll be amazed! We were.

We wanted to see the Mystery House, but time was ticking. We did have time, though, to buy souvenirs and doodads, and then we visited "Big Mo." Oh, what is "Big Mo," well, it is a mosasaur fossil. I even posed with the full-scale replica of the ancient beast that they have out front.

Time for the caves.

Part 13

I may have written this already about the trip to Memphis but will write it again. Everything went smoothly, even going to Mammoth Cave. We arrived just in time for the tour to start, and I mean, just in time.

We hurriedly bought tickets for the "Domes and Dripstones" tour. Big Mikes Rock Shop recommended it. This cave tour was rated as moderate for the effort even though it has a descent of 280 steps down and about a hundred more steps in various places. It shows the Frozen Niagara, one of the main highlights of Mammoth Caves, and is two hours long.

The park ranger/guide allowed us a few extra minutes to run to the restroom, if needed and grab water and light jackets which he suggested. I sprinted to the Go-Go Bus, got three jackets, some water, and unloaded my pockets. I could just imagine dropping my wallet or phone in some deep crevice, so those items were staying secure locked up in the Bus.

I ran all the way back to where they started to line up for the tour bus that takes people over to the cave entrance. I caught up with Ruth and Paul, they hand their ticket to the bus driver, I reach for mine and "Umm, sir, my ticket is in my wallet, and my wallet is in my vehicle." Good thing the ranger/guide who took my money minutes earlier vouched for me that I paid. I was allowed on with no ticket.

It was about a ten-minute drive to the entrance. During the ride, our guide gave us facts and some FYI about Mammoth Cave.

It is the largest cave system in the world. More than 400 miles of it have been discovered and explored. It is one of the oldest tourist attractions in North America, with tours being offered since 1816. He asked if there were any questions. I raised my hand and asked what about cave-ins? He responded, "We don't like to call them cave-ins, but sinkholes have developed, however you are safe."

The park was heavily wooded. Our guide noted what animals and birds we might see. One of them was the turkey. Almost as if on cue, a turkey flew in front of the bus, right across the road. We were almost at our destination, so the guide asked, "Any more questions before we leave? I raised my hand and asked, "YES, I DO. Why did the turkey cross the road?" I got no response or chuckle from anyone except Paul, not even from Ruth; well from her, I got an elbow in my ribs.

Part 14

OK, I am back. Sorry to leave you in the dark, but not as in the dark as the cave tour we took.

We were given brief instructions on what we could bring and things we couldn't.

Cameras and video cameras were allowed, but no flash. It was explained the reason is, not because of the caves, but because when the flash goes off, people were complaining they got blinded. Oh boy!

After instructions, it was a long descent down. Most everyone in the crowd was oohing and ahing and just having a good time. At the bottom of the stairs, the cave opened into a fairly large room. The room was set up with benches. The guide made everyone sit down and take a break to get acclimated to the cave.

Paul nudged me and said, "Carey, I am not well, not feeling good." I felt so bad for him. He said, go on without me. One of the guides brought him to the surface to wait while Ruth and I finished the tour.

Paul still wasn't sure what caused him to feel ill. Was it the rapid descent, or his mind racing with what with what if it did cave in as I said earlier; me and my big mouth.

One little boy, though, was having the time of his life. He kept asking, where is Batman? When a real bat flew around overhead, instead of freaking, he laughed and shouted, "There's Batman"! What a sport.

Part 15

In summary of Mammoth Cave – it is not as live as other caves I toured. I found sections were not that impressive when compared to caves such as Luray Caverns. Nonetheless it is still very much worth a visit.

On the way to the Mammoth Cave, it started to lightly drizzle. By the time the bus brought us back to the welcome center, it was raining and never really stopped until late Monday. Before that, it was picture-perfect weather for the entire trip.

The welcome center had a really fascinating and informative exhibit set up showcasing the early history of Cave Country and the caves' discovery. Even if you don't tour the caves, the exhibit should be seen.

Paul found us. He looked refreshed and ready to go. Whatever happened to him, it was nothing serious. We were all hungry, so it was time to leave and head back for supper.

Sorry, but here is another sad commentary on America. In years past, one thing you could usually find was quality meat in the little town. The reason was that many of the local stores got their meat from the local farmer. For instance, when I used to frequent Rocky Fork in Ohio, I would always go to this gas station food mart. They had the best small meat counter. All the meat was local. Today it is hard to find the little independent place as we found on this trip. We eventually spotted a Save A Lot and went there.

The meat didn't look the best, so we quickly left and located another grocery store in town that was a little better. I found an item in this store that brought a smile and a remembrance of past travels down south—a hanging smoked ham. Most grocery stores or similar places in the Virginia, Tennessee, and Kentucky region, maybe other states also, usually had, and I guess still do, netted or bagged smoked hams hanging from the ceiling or a pole. The bagged ham I found at this food store was hanging on a pole by laundry soap, making it look less appealing. Unless the connection, an ad that promises "For that clean smoked ham taste try..."

During our search for a grocery store, we came upon Tepee Village motel. Talk about another throwback to the old roadside America days. According to the motel website, there was a chain of them. Only three exist now. This one in Kentucky dated back to 1936.

Because of the time and rain, we decided to put our groceries on ice and have our last supper at Look Out restaurant. I will leave you hanging like a smoked ham and finish this later

Part 16

We had our last supper at the hotel. The food was again average at best. After we ate, I hung around and used the laptop to write, and the rest went to their rooms. A man walked in and headed towards the desk. I said "The desk staff will be right back." He asked if our room was hot. I told him the air conditioning was seasonal and not turned on yet, but they would bring a fan to your room if you like. I could tell the front desk when they return. He then approached me and properly introduced himself. His name was John. He served in Iraq and, after an injury, was sent home. The reason for his visit to this area was a turkey hunt to benefit Wounded Warriors. After he experienced a spell of feeling sorry for himself, his wife encouraged him to get active and get involved, so he joined that organization.

The desk clerk came back, so I told him about John needing a fan. I stuck around the desk for a while. The staff told me more details and stories of the hotel. The hotel was the place to stay in the early days, with many wealthy patrons returning year after year. Locals would just show up at the entrance to be porters and work for tips. I also learned that on the grounds are caves, but the government has shut them. One cave was closed because of a bat colony, and another because of a salamander.

While we were talking, the TV in the lobby had repeated weather warnings going on—severe weather with possible tornados for the surrounding area and neighboring states.

After the conversation, I made it to the Go-Go Bus just in time. Then the rains came, and it rained and rained hard. I napped and awoke to high winds and a siren. I jumped and yelled to Ruth, "I think it's a tornado siren going off", but it quickly ended. Still not sure if it was a tornado warning or a police siren. It stopped so I fell back to sleep.

Part 17

We had breakfast and loaded up. It was time to head out. I was sad to leave; I really started liking the place more and more each day.

It was fairly early, so I avoided the freeway and found a scenic route heading north. From Park City, I drove 31-W, heading northeast into Cave City. I know W should mean west but not on this route.

Cave City didn't keep up with the times or continue promoting the caves nearby nearly enough. Main Street's original businesses are closed and now filled with antique shops. It is like so many other towns trying to fill empty stores.

The second-hand store that got our attention was Magaline's Antique Mall. There were billboards in and around Cave City showing a smiling lady wearing a Victorian-style hat advertising Magaline's. The signs were so hokey and homey we had to stop, and we did.

As we entered the store, there they were, the owners Magaline and her husband. And yes, she did dress just like the way she looked in the signs advertising her store. Both of them were so hospitable and helpful. They had a variety of mostly old items but newer merchandise could also be found.

Dan and Paul finished their browsing and shopping. The husband offered chairs then sat with them, conversing like old friends while Ruth and I continued our shopping. We even snuck off and went to other antique stores in town, leaving them behind. When we got back, they were still talking. It was time to leave. We were told the best route north for scenery was 70 to 31-E or N Jackson Highway, the other name for the routes, I assume E is for east and N is for north, so why both weren't labeled one or the other is beyond me. Again I was confused by all this route trickery.

The route they suggested goes right by the Lincoln Memorial National Park, Sinking Spring Farm, the birthplace of Abraham Lincoln in Hodgenville, Kentucky. We made it to the memorial in great time, and just as the rain had stopped.

The Lincoln Memorial was an odd memorial. At least to me, it was. It didn't blend in with the surrounding area, which was mostly wooded. As you entered the park, you saw in the distance a stone structure, something such as you might see in Greece. The memorial was built on a hill with a large number of steps leading up to it. Very impressive, but it seemed out of place. I found out later there were 56 steps, signifying the age of Abraham Lincoln when he died.

Inside, the elaborate Greek mausoleum-like structure gets even odder. All that is in there is a reproduction of Abraham's cabin that he was born in. The visitor center is excellent, and there are short walking trails to various landmarks, including Sinking Spring.

The second to last stop before hitting the road to start the trek home was visiting the city of Hodgenville itself, a neat little city with a quaint downtown. After browsing the shops and stores, we started back to the

Go-Go Bus, when I noticed a sign in a window of an insurance business, J. Alex LaRue, Republican candidate for State Representative. I told Ruth, Dan, and Paul, I will catch up to you; I wanted to grab a flier. Just as I was about to walk in, I saw J. Alex LaRue himself walk out. I introduced myself. He said, "Go on in, I will be right back."

When LaRue returned, we went to his office and chatted for a while. I didn't think it was that long, but Ruth, Dan, and Paul sure did. They were a bit upset and angered that I said I would be right back. I said, "Well, it seems you put the lost time to good use. I see all of you have milkshakes." They spied an ice cream/candy store across the street called Sweet Shoppe, which is excellent. I told them, "If I had walked back with you and not talked, you would have never found that tasty treat."

That concluded our trip all but the eight more hours of drive time home that went by uneventfully.

OH wait… the gas cap, I need to tell you about the gas cap. Somewhere before Washington Courthouse, Ohio on Rt. 71 heading to Tennessee, I stopped for gas. And somewhere in Kentucky, on my next fill-up, I noticed I forgot to put on my gas cap. Needless to write, I was not happy. Gas could easily evaporate, and finding a good replacement cap for a '69 would be difficult. I used aluminum foil and a rubber band for the entire trip. When we crossed back over to Ohio on the return trip, I prayed that the cap would be there. I retraced my steps to the gas station where I filled up 6 days earlier. As I am pulling into the gas station, there was my gas cap, still sitting on top of the pump. It was an answered prayer that capped a happy ending to a memorable trip.

Chapter Six

The Trip to See God

In 1987 in the town of Tickfaw, Louisiana, a vision of St. Joseph appeared in an onion field.

Though, to this day, I still wonder whether the masses who gathered were tearing from actually seeing St. Joseph or because they were standing in an onion field. We may never be able to answer that question, but I can for sure tell you about my trip to see God.

This was one of the most fun and unusual spontaneous jaunts I have ever taken. It even beats the time around midnight after the Cleveland Auto-Rama with some friends, and one asking about Niagara Falls in the winter. I said OK, let's go. And off we went to get a chunk of ice off the falls, and sure enough, we did. Sadly the ice melted in the bucket on the way home.

Anyway, now about this adventure to see God, let's rewind back, way back to 1986.

Rick told me to meet him at Groves Town Bar in Wickliffe. When I arrived, it was past 11:00 p.m. Rick was the only customer in the place, sitting there at the bar, drinking a beer, and watching the news on the small TV that was hoisted up in the corner.

As I walk in and approach him, a news story caught my attention. Rick tried to say hi, but I quickly shooshed him, wait, let me hear this. All I caught was in Fostoria, Ohio, people saw a vision of God on a soybean oil tank. I said, well, let's go. I know where we are going and what we are doing. We are going to Fostoria to see God, and just like that, off we went.

Before embarking, the car was gassed up, but I didn't let on to Rick that I used all my cash in doing so. And he told me beforehand that he didn't have anything to contribute to the trip; he spent his last few bucks on beer. But that little detail of having no money didn't deter me or dampen my spirit for a road trip to see this heavenly vision. Not until we were close to the exit on the toll road the detail of no funds was revealed to Rick.

Rick, we need to get off at this rest area to panhandle some cash for the toll road. Huh? Well, I don't have any money left to pay the toll. We can't exit without paying. So that's what we did, panhandled and exited.

Rick has a way of taking a bad or trying situation, and without getting upset, he exploits it humorously. So instead of going up to random people as I was asking for spare change and making up a fib of a lost wallet and money, Rick was walking around and talking loudly to everyone he saw, "We are going to see God. We need money. Can you help us go see God"? Sure enough, in no time, our charity show gathered enough income to exit the toll road and proceed on our journey to the Godly silo.

This same scenario played out on our return trip. We needed more toll and gas money. Rick once again, went into his routine, except this time he was barking, "We just saw God, can you help us get home? We need gas. We just saw God. Please help!" And sure enough, people contributed quarters and dollars to our cause of making it back home, or maybe they gave money to get us away from them.

We arrived in Fostoria way past midnight into the early a.m. Once in the town, we asked someone where to go. They sure told us. We found the location, pulled off the road like the other cars gathered, and joined the spectators. It didn't matter how late it was. Plenty of people were still out. The atmosphere was party-like, nothing religious about it. Everyone was talking to each other, sharing their thoughts, it was like a freak show at the circus.

So did I see God? No, and I was frustrated and mad. I tried every which way to find the apparition. I tilted my head to the left, to the right, closed one eye, squinted, nothing, no vision, all that distance, and no sighting. According to everyone else gathered there, including Rick, they said they saw something but not me. I wish I could tell you otherwise. I know it's anticlimactic, but I can't lie. I saw nothing.

Though I can tell you about the man next to us who saw the ghostly vision. He swore it didn't look like God, but Buckwheat from the Little Rascals. Soybean tanker – buckwheat, I sort of see the connection.

This was the first time I traveled to see a vision. The second time I went to see Mother Mary on an office building in Orlando, Florida. And once again, I didn't see her either, but that's another story for another time for another book.

The Anxiety Group

I attended with a friend a support group
for people with anxiety and nervousness.
When the meeting came to a close, the
leader said "Coffee and refreshments
for those wanting to hang around and
chat." My immediate thought was this:
These people are already nervous.
Should they really be drinking coffee?

Chapter Seven

The Outing to the Christmas Story House, From the Movie The Christmas Story Cleveland, Ohio

Have you ever had one of those moments where nothing went right, then everything turned out just perfect? That's what I thought – I knew you could relate.

This is how our Sunday outing started off. I was still getting ready when Mike, Adrianne, and Doug arrived on time. What is wrong with people? There is nothing worse than having people arrive when they are supposed to. So I hurry up to start the ordeal of moving my cars around to pull out the vehicle we would be driving. I was nominated to be the driver and use my van.

First in line at the end of the drive was my car. I pulled that in the street and left it running. Next up was my work van. The thing is falling apart. It is down to one door that works, and that is the sliding side door. I get in, lock it as I climbed into the driver's seat. Errer errer errer, and that's what it sounded like. The ole' Astro just wouldn't crank. I jump out and immediately realize, OH NO, the key is in the ignition, and no doors work, so even a slimjim won't help. I panicked again when I realized my spare key is locked inside also.

I go back to my other van that Mike, Adrianne, and Doug are now sitting in, waiting for me. Don't worry, the van won't start, but we can push it out. Let me get the spare key. If they had known how I really felt at the time, they would have worried. I went to look for the spare key inside the house, just hoping, really hoping I was wrong and they were inside the house. They weren't. Now what? Well, here are the keys for my parents Chevy, let's try that. And believe it or not, they worked. I was able to unlock the side door of the Astro.

When I asked Mike to help push the dead van out of the way, he replied: "Carey, I can't push. I'm dressed too nice." So Doug and I pushed while Mike steered the van to the backyard. We get in my other van, and as I am backing up, we hear a loud POP. I ran over a trash bag with a bottle in it. Glass went everywhere but luckily, no flat tire. After sweeping up, I am out of the drive about to zoom off when I realized while looking back that I left my car in the street with the engine still running. So put the van in reverse, jump out, and pull my car into the drive. That's how the outing to see the Christmas Story House began.

By the way, did you follow all of that?

Cleveland, the city I once knew, has changed so drastically that I really don't know my way around anymore. The Innerbelt Bridge has been reconfigured, structures are missing, and the Christmas Story House location in Tremont has also changed. Houses are being torn down or refurbished, people walking and jogging, some upscale boutiques and restaurants; it's livelier, a real transformation. Back in the day, when I used to hang around, it was for drunks, punks, and the poor but not anymore. Shall we say gentrification? Finally, I get to use that word in a sentence, thank you May. Who's May? Well, she is the woman who explained gentrification to me.

I exit at W. 11th, which is one of the streets the Christmas Story House is near. But we couldn't find the house. The reason is W. 11th is divided in two; we had to find the other half. Mike rolled down the window and asked a man walking, "Where is the Christmas Story House?" He explained, we needed to drive around. He then told us what streets to take to get to the other side. Or, (here comes the or, I didn't learn my lesson from Letchworth, read my second book, you'll understand) he said as he was pointing, "Why don't you just park here and use that footbridge? It will take you across to the house. That might be easier".

I asked Adrienne's mom, who is elderly, if she was able to walk, "Sure, I feel fine, I can walk." So I park the van, and off we went, over the footbridge and through no snow and over the freeway we go. All was fine until we got to a fork in the road. You had to know that was coming. One path went up – literally. Doug, Adrienne's husband, was concerned about his mom-in-law and was not happy we had to walk this far, and who knew how much farther. He was all in favor waiting right there as I walked to get the van.

I volunteered to climb and scout the high road while they stayed put. I came down with this report, no Christmas Story House up there, so it must be the low road. Doug insisted a bit louder, "We should turn back and drive." I said, "Wait, I think I see the house. Let's continue". What I saw was a house with Christmas lights, why couldn't that be it? But it wasn't.

Mike and I briskly walked ahead, trying to get a glimpse of some landmark, sign, or other that indeed showed we were on the right path. Just then, a cop car appears. I flag it down and ask, "How far is the Christmas Story house?" The reply was it's still a good walk. I said, "Following behind us is an 83-year-old lady. Could you please give her a ride, please"! Before he could get his mouth open to say anything, I was thanking him for being a blessing. The cop was more than happy to play chauffeur. I chased after the patrol car as it pulled in front of Adrienne,

Doug, and Mom. I was yelling, "It's OK, don't worry, we didn't do anything wrong, they will give you a ride," and they did.

Adrienne and Mom rode in the car, Doug, Mike, and I walked behind. I called them the Angels in Blue. When I caught up to Adrienne and her Mom, I teased, "See, I told you I would get you here and not only that but a free ride in a cop car." I thanked the patrolman again. He said, "After I am done ordering my food at this stand, I will give you a ride back to get your van now. You don't want to walk that far after the tour, it will be no problem. We will give you a ride". I then asked his name. Patrolman Dooley was his name. What a gentleman. That's how a policeman should act. Adrienne, Mom, Doug, and Mike stood in line for the tour as I left with the cop.

We made small talk on the way to my van. Patrolman Dooley agreed with my assessment of how our society is crumbling and America needs a morality check. I told him I would make sure to let others know how kind Patrolman Dooley and his partner were. He replied back, "Right now, we need all the good publicity we could get." I was about to jump out of the patrol car, but his kindness was not done yet. He said, "Just follow us. We will lead you back". What a blessing.

With the police guidance, I parked only a block away from the Christmas Story House. As I was getting out of my van, so was a man just getting out of his car. He asked me, "Do you think we can park here?" I answered back, "I was going to ask you, but I assume we can since others are." He was from Illinois, so I welcomed him to Ohio. Even with the help from the cops, I was still spun around, so I asked the man, "Which direction is the house?" According to my GPS, he said, "Take a left here. I know this is the street because I laughed when I saw the sign – Rawley, that's my last

54

name, can you take a photo of me under the street sign, Rawley?" That was weird. What's the chance of running into a Rawley directly under a Rawley street sign?

When I met back up with the gang, they had slowly moved ahead in line. Earlier, the line went around the block, so my episode of getting the van was not a waste of time; while they stood, I was occupied. Again I teased Adrienne's mom about being in the back of the police car and asked if she had flashbacks from her earlier life of crime. Relax, she's not an ex-con, well, at least not that I know.

Well, What About the Christmas Story House – OH YEAH!

If you are a lover or fan of the movie "The Christmas Story" and want to see what a house looked like during the 1940's it is well worth it, a must-see. I went twice in different years during the Christmas season. I enjoyed it both times. The crowd is into it, which makes for a festive holiday atmosphere.

Across the street from the Christmas Story house is a museum. It showcases trivia and some props from the movie. It's right next to a souvenir shop selling various Christmas movie memorabilia and other fun gifts. All of this combined makes a perfect Christmas outing. I rate it high on fun, but just don't take the footbridge.

Chapter Eight

'tis the Season to Remember

Since we just left the Christmas Story House let's stay with the festive spirit. There really is no other time of year that recalls so many fond memories as does Christmas. I could probably write an entire book just on the Christmas season.

So I'd like to share with you a few tips on what not to do to ensure the holiday season is memorable in a good way and not for the wrong reason.

Let's start with presents.

Christmas Gifts - What Not to Buy

Take my advice and do not buy these things as gifts.

Number one on the list is a toilet seat. I bought one for my friend Pam. Oh my, did it ruin the party and almost cost a friendship. A simple toilet seat, I never expected it to cause such a commotion. I still don't understand why she cried and wouldn't accept it. I tried telling her how practical a gift a toilet seat was. You can use it year-round, other people will use it, and you will think of me every time you sit on it. It didn't matter what I said. She wouldn't talk to me the rest of the night, and I had to take it back.

Number two is a spider, a hairy tarantula, to be exact. I gave the tarantula to Liz during our Christmas Eve celebration. She wasn't too keen on a large fuzzy crawling pet, but she accepted it anyway. That wasn't the problem. Mayhem ensued when Liz got home from the party and placed the container with the spider on her kitchen table. Her brother woke up in the middle of the night to relieve himself, then he went into the kitchen to grab a snack. He saw the container on the table and, thinking it was cookies, reached in, and what followed were shrieks of terror. Can you imagine being half asleep and almost grabbing a tarantula?

What occurred next was just as bad or worse. Early Christmas morning, someone was pounding on my front door. Dad jumped up, startled, and ran to see who was there and what emergency it was. He was greeted by Liz's Mom threatening my life and shouting Carey ruined my Christmas. He gave Liz a spider as a gift. Dad was bewildered, not knowing what was going on. I was scared, so I hid. After an hour, things calmed down.

So number two on our shortlist is – don't give giant spiders and exotic animals as presents and no toilet seats.

Liz looking overly enthused with Harry the tarantula

Stay Away From Food Coloring

I gave you two good tips on what not to give and now a recommendation on what not to serve: blue mashed potatoes.

Poor Pam, this is another story of how I traumatized her.

I got this clever idea from my sister Candi. She use to make mashed potatoes and add some red food coloring. It made dinner fun and colorful.

Anyway, Pam was all excited because she was attending culinary school. She wanted to cook dinner for our Christmas party. It was her first big meal, pot roast, mashed potatoes, and all the fixings that go with it.

I thought I should make it festive. Remembering what my sister use to do, I insisted on adding blue food coloring to the mashed potatoes. Pam was perturbed that I was toying with her recipe and food. Listen, don't worry, it will be fun. Pam relented, so I added a few drops, not enough, some more drops and some more and some more. Pam was now upset to the point of tears. OH OH. It didn't matter the dinner tasted great. She only focused on the one person who didn't want to eat the potatoes because of how they looked and how everyone else's teeth and lips turned blue. Sadly it made for a blue occasion, poor Pam, she cried again. I never touched her food after that.

Chapter Nine

Bennigan's and Carey, Carey & Karrie
No It's Not a Law Firm

I told you this book is going back to the archives, here is another from the vault. This story is about Bennigan's restaurant when they were in the Cleveland, Ohio area more than a few years ago.

It is about how I landed the Bennigan's restaurant janitorial account for my cleaning business; it was as if it was planned, or maybe it was.

I just got off work when Jeff M, whom I haven't seen in some time, called. He wanted to take me out to IHOP for dinner. Of course, I accepted the invitation without asking questions.

I drove over to pick him up, and he said, why don't we go to TJ's in Mentor instead.

So we head to TJ's but bypass it because once more, our destination was changed. Now we were thinking of driving way out to Fairport. But then Jeff M. suddenly changed his mind for the fourth time and said, nah, that's too far, let's turn around and stick to our second choice TJ's.

We were just about finished with our TJ's dinner when I called Allen to see what he, Jeff B. , and Chris were doing. It just so happened the trio was at Bennigan's right down the street. I was surprised they drove out to Mentor instead of eating closer to where they live. Jeff M. paid the bill, and we quickly left.

We joined our friends at Bennigan's. Over silly conversation trying to figure out where we would go next, Jeff M. started flirting with the waitress. He asked who cleans the carpet here. I thought to myself, some pick-up line, huh? She said I'll send the manager over. And his name was – Carey. Immediately I went from being silly to the persona of a business owner. I gave him a quote right there. He said you definitely have the edge over everyone else because of your name. I called a few days later and, sure enough, landed the account.

Isn't that neat?

A Conversation at Bennigans

This happened while I was cleaning Bennigan's carpet a month later. The pump-up sprayer's nozzle that is used to spray the cleaner was clogged. It needed a pin or paper clip to clear it. I approached a waitress.

"Excuse me, do you have a paper clip"? "No, we don't have paper cups." "No, I said a paper clip." "That's what I said, we don't have paper cups." "No, a paper C - L - I - P!" "That's what I said, we don't have paper cups." She yelled at a coworker, "Can you show him the cups we have." I said listen, "PAPER CLIP, PAAAAPER CLIIIIIIP." "Oh, I'm sorry, thought you said paper cup." "Well, do you have one?" "No, they're up in the office, follow me."

We go to the office and Carey, the manager, is there. The waitress announces he needs a paper clip. He said, "I don't have any." I asked, "Do you have anything pointy, a pin?" "Here, you could use this safety pin, would that work?" "Yes, do you need it back?" "Of course, it's my spare key."

Just then, another waitress walks in.

Manager Carey asked, "So Karrie, how did you do on tips?" I interrupt, "You're Carey also, C-a-r-e-y?" "No Karrie K-A-R-R-I-E." The manager Carey, tells Karrie, "Yes, he's Carey also." She said, "Really, you're Carey?" I said, "Yes, and that's scary."

Why is the weather called Mother Nature? Because just like a woman, the weather has hot flashes, cold spells and overall is unstable. Whereas if it was Father Nature it would be a constant 60 degrees with 12 months of football.

Chapter Ten

Ooh That Smell

In all of my stories, I use real first names and sometimes full names. But in this story, to avoid embarrassment to the person it is about, I will use a fictitious name. And to be honest, it will save me from a good beating. So the name I will use is Nadine. I don't think I know a Nadine. I hope I don't.

Nadine calls and asks, "Hey can you do me a favor?" "Sure, what is it?" "I need to do a few errands, and I need someone to watch the kids." Um…" Don't worry, you won't have to do a thing, they're in bed." "Uh, what about diaper changing, bottles?" "I won't be that long. You will be OK, trust me."

I head over to Nadine's. She greets me at the door with a big thank you. As I walk in, an odor introduced itself with a hello and a smack on my back." WOW, what is that smell?" It smelled so bad of dirty diapers and whatnot. It was atrocious. I said, "Where is the air freshener?" "I'm sorry, I don't have any." "What about candles? This is obnoxious". "Sorry, no candles, I need to leave, will hurry right back." "Wait!"

I was not about to sit in this apartment with the odor from beyond. Something had to be done. I rummaged through all the cupboards, closets, nothing that I could use. I even looked in the fridge, slammed it shut, opened it again, and it came to me, AHA! I can use that this will make the place smell good.

So I turned on all the lamps and lights in the apartment, then went back to the fridge, sliced an onion, grabbed the sliced pickles, ketchup, and mustard. Then I went to work. Carefully I placed a slice of onion, a pickle slice, and a drizzle of ketchup and mustard on each light bulb. In no time, the place started smelling better. The heat from the bulbs gave the condiments an aroma of cooking on a grill. It even made me hungry.

Nadine comes home, steps inside, and immediately says, "What are you cooking? It smells so good in here". I said, "Nothing; I am deodorizing your house." Huh! I showed her what I did. Well, she didn't know what to say other than WHAT!

She got over it, well after she scrubbed all her light bulbs clean, and well, I was never asked to watch her kids again. Not sure why?

Ya just never know who you'll run into.
Today, for instance, I ran into
my neighbor's car.

Chapter Eleven

Short Ones
Really I'm not Blond or Senile
But I Do Know How to Laugh at Myself

Walt invited me to the Heisley Racket Club. His son Jimmy challenged me to a match which I accepted. As we were playing, I couldn't figure out why the ball wasn't going straight and why I wasn't getting enough power out of my swing. We finished our game, and as we left the court, I looked at my racket. DUH, I forgot to take it out of its case. I played the entire time with the cover still on my racket. But hey, just don't laugh at me, Jimmy never noticed it either, unless he did… that rat!

The Party

My sister Cynthia was hosting a Christmas party. I was greeting people as they entered. A couple came in with a tray. I introduced myself, and the reply back as they handed it to me was salmon patties.

I thought to myself, strange plate to bring but not wanting them to feel bad, said, "Oh salmon patties, I will have to try one."

The man said, "Huh? Salmon patties? It's a dessert!"

"Um, didn't you say salmon patties?"

"NO, I said we're SAM and PATTY."

"OH well, pleased to meet you."

Here's one more name game, or is it more like a fish tale?

Dave and Sherry's Wedding Reception

I was directed to the table and seat I was assigned to. Sat down and introduced myself to the man sitting across from me. I told him my name but had a hard time pronouncing the name written on the sign in front of him. Over and over, I tried, and all the man did was smile and chuckle. I asked, "Well, is it a French name?" Trying to pronounce it phonetically, I said again, "Gre 'led Samoan?" Again a smile and a chuckle were returned. No use. He was not helping me. So I adjusted my paper name tag sign and noticed mine said baked chicken. It wasn't a sign for our names but what we were eating. The man was eating grilled salmon.

I never play any April Fools' jokes.
It's the one day of the year I am serious.
This fools people.

Chapter Twelve

Wake in a Park

What was supposed to be a somber memorial event turned into one mishap and hilarity after another. We will have to return to spread the ashes of Mom Robey.

I am sure she is looking down and saying, yep, that's my boys and Noelle, well, you got your exercise.

So what could possibly go wrong with having an intimate memorial service in a park? Plenty!

Sunday was the scheduled day to scatter Bruce's Mom's ashes. Plans were to meet at Bruce's house and then drive separately to Indian Point, the place Mom requested.

Some FYI, I hope you don't mind a commercial in the middle of a story.

"Indian Point" is located in Leroy, Ohio, and part of Lake Metroparks. It has a 100-foot tall ridge that overlooks the Grand River and Paine Creek. It also has a 15-foot double-decker waterfall that's off the trail in the woods.

I don't think it was rude to throw that in because I am reasonably certain you asked yourself, what is Indian Point?

Now you know, and now back to the story…

Right off, things went south. Bruce invited Noelle, his cousin, and me in. He had blueberry pie ready to snack on while he gave us some of Mom's jewelry he wanted us to have. We eagerly accepted the keepsakes, but his cousin, Noelle, because of health reasons, can't have any pastries, and I have a wheat intolerance. I guess those are both health reasons, huh? Not wanting him to feel bad, I ate half a slice. After that, it was off to Indian Point.

Bruce leads the way, Noel is second in her car, and I am bringing up the rear in my van. For some unknown reason, Bruce took an indirect route that got us all scrambled. We have been to this park many times, but that was many years ago. Since then, roads have widened, landmarks and gas stations razed, so I can understand getting mixed up and lost even though I still don't know why he chose that way.

Bruce pulls into another park which I think he thought was Indian Point, but it wasn't. He asks do you know where it is. Noelle spins her car around and says, "Hello, I have GPS!" I answer back, "No, that's cheating. Follow me." The shuffled lineup now had me in the lead, Bruce next with Noelle in the back. I head in the reverse direction that we just drove, looking for the landmark gas station that has disappeared. I end up back in Mentor. I turn around in someone's drive that is having a mini foreign car show in his yard. I ask him Hey do you know how to get to Indian Point? He gave somewhat of a direction and said once there, ask someone else. I shouted this back to Bruce and Noelle with a follow me. Noelle once more repeated loudly, "HELLO, I HAVE GPS!" which, of course, I ignored yet again.

Following the directions, the gentleman with the foreign car show just told us I speed off. Bruce catches up with Noelle on his tail. All was going fine until I get to this roundabout. I hate roundabouts. Why are they putting them in everywhere? What was wrong with the four-way stop? Are we going to do away with crossroads? At a four-way, everyone stops, looks at each other, then one car at a time goes. This has been going on for years since crossroads were invented during the dirt trail days. These stupid roundabouts are like a bad amusement park ride.

Well, I got disoriented. This whole little excursion was like the disoriented express. I tell Bruce and Noelle, who followed me into this parking lot, umm, I am not sure where I am. What does Noelle say? Come on, you know. "Hello, I HAVE GPS!" OK, I give up. You take the lead. Her GPS had us backtrack a bit and onto another road that I was not familiar with. In the distance, there was a park. This has to be it. Nope, the sign read Paine Falls Park, another park, and another wrong park. Back on the road, down a gravel dirt road that was kicking up a dust storm, which led us to our destination Indian Point.

Both Bruce and I were puzzled again; this sure didn't look like the entrance we remembered. Wow, have things changed. Later, we found out that when the new bridge was built, the old entrance is no longer accessible, it's gone, no longer there, poof, erased, just a memory. Did I elaborate too much?

Now let me try to set this next scene for you so you can picture it. Indian Point is woodsy with trails, not a very developed park, mostly natural in its setting. Bruce is dressed as Bruce usually dresses, jeans, and a T-shirt. Noelle had on a long black dress that looked to me like she was going to sing at an opera. Noelle corrected me and said, "It was actually a long skirt with a studded shirt, all black, I didn't know I needed hiking clothes that day lol, thought it was a little walk and was doing the proper clothing for a so-called wake." OK, thank you, Noelle. Aren't you proud you have contributed to the writing of this book? I was sporting a casual black shirt, casual dress shorts topped with a 1960's Richmond Bros. black straw hat with a two-inch gray and red band. I was definitely dressed for a wake in the park.

We use the restrooms, and then Bruce anxiously and hurriedly hits the trail with the box of his Mom's remains under his arm. I being a gentleman, decided to simmer my jets and walk with Noelle, who was using her walker. It was reminiscent of the tale of the tortoise and the hare. Every time we caught up to Bruce, he would spring up from a park bench or sitting on the trail and take off again.

It was a sight. Noelle looking like an opera singer, huffing and clinging to her walker. I'm attired nicely and carrying my eulogy in a plastic folder with hikers coming and going passing us. I decided to have fun with all of this. When a group passed us on the trail, I would speak up loudly and say, "OK, Noelle let's pick it up. When we get to our destination, I want you to drop down and give me 10 pushups"! I was acting like I was her trainer. Two older ladies laughed with one saying, "Oh, I don't think she is going to make it. She is sitting, sir, but I do like your hat." Another male jogger gave us an update jogging to and from, "You have a good distance to go yet" on the return, "I really don't think she is going to make it, I am 53, and it was hard for me".

In the meantime, Bruce was sitting again and took a smoke break. He forgot cigarettes, so he decided to roll leaves to smoke. I had to throw that in; I mean, how many people do you see smoking tree leaves?

Finally, we arrived almost at the location Bruce chose. Why almost? Noelle was just not going to make it the rest of the way. We stopped at the very first overlook.

It was now time to change gears and get into a more serious mode for the reason why we were here. We took a deep breath, got quiet, reflected for a moment. I cleared my throat and spoke first.

I read what I had written. Noelle said a few words, and Bruce concluded the ceremony. We took another breath, collected ourselves, a brief moment of silence, and then Bruce opened the box. WHAT! I am not sure who said what first, or maybe it was a collective what, but I do know, we all had the same puzzled look. The box contained a plaque, not ashes. I blurted out with the first thing that crossed my mind, "Oh my goodness, they pressed her into a plaque!" Bruce was stunned. Noelle said, "Well, they have been making people's ashes into different things like glass, so maybe they did." The color of the plaque also threw us off; it was like grayish beige. Noelle grabbed the plaque and quickly ended that speculation. On the backside, it had a tag that read made in China. I said that's definitely not her, she was born in Iowa. Noelle corrected me and said Missouri.

Bruce kept on apologizing and said, "But what would you think? It says on the box personalization, am I right? Doesn't it say personalization?" Noelle spoke up and said, "Personalization is the name of the company, it didn't mean her remains! It's a personal memorial plaque for Aunt June." "Well, I didn't know. I received this box in the mail." "They don't mail remains. You have to pick them up at the funeral home and sign for them!"

After bewilderment, confusion, and exchange of unpleasantries, we calmed down and made tentative plans to return to redo the entire ceremony.

Was that the end of this ordeal? No, there was still the task of walking the long distance back to our cars. Bruce was ready to hightail, I wanted to zoom back, but Noelle was quite worn out. I was not about to leave Noelle in the dust all by herself. Squabbling back and forth about what to do, I spoke up and said, "I know, Bruce, let's get your car and drive back while Noelle waits here. Your car will easily fit on the trails." Bruce's car is the Chevy Spark which is smaller than a Mini Cooper or slightly larger than a full-grown Great Dane.

So that's what we did, hurried to Bruce's car, jumped in, maneuvered past the sign that said "NO MOTORIZED VEHICLES PAST THIS POINT," and off-roaded towards Noelle. Bumpity bump bump Bruce was flying. This was no leisurely drive. We get to Noelle, and round two happens. Insert colorful language here. Get in the car! My walker. I can't get the trunk open. I am going to walk. Thinking he is going to get arrested, Bruce panics. Insert more colorful language here. The trunk is opened, walker thrown in, I take the back seat, Bruce and Noelle get in, and we're off – Indian Point Baha part two. Slow down. I am not slowing down. I am not going to get arrested. Slow down. You almost hit a hiker. Where. They were on the side of the trail. I didn't see any hiker. Slow down. Insert some more colorful language here. I am not slowing down. Did you ever think of painting your car green and start a Uber for stranded hikers?

Back in the parking lot, everyone calmed down, made plans to return, said our goodbyes, and drove off. I took a different direction driving out of the park and ended up close to the roundabout that threw me off course. Who needs GPS? I get lost and found just fine without it.

Chapter Thirteen

Pow Wow Wow

This is a story of being at the right place at the right time. I may always be late, but I'm always there at the right time. Actually, maybe not as I have been many times in the wrong place at the right time, or is it the wrong place at the wrong time, I'm not sure, but this account is about right and right – place and time.

It is a story about how I was adopted by an American Indian family for a day. Not a very long narrative but nonetheless definitely one of the more unique experiences I've had. Reflecting back, I realize how truly blessed I was to participate in this event.

Rick and I took off for a day trip starting in Erie, Pennsylvania, the Presque Isle area. After driving across the peninsula, we headed east to Salamanca, New York, with no real destination in mind when we encountered a broken-down mini-school bus on the edge of town.

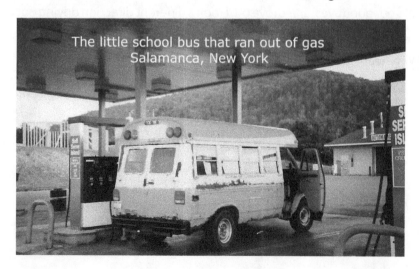

The little school bus that ran out of gas
Salamanca, New York

The mini-school bus was being pushed by kids and a lady while another lady was steering. I immediately pulled off the road. Rick and I ran up to the bus to lend a hand. They had run out of gas and were trying to get it to a gas station that was still a good 25 yards or so away.

When the bus was safe beside the gas pump, instead of a quick thank you, the ladies were so thankful for our kindness they invited us to attend a Pow Wow they were heading to.

Leta driver of the mini-school bus
Pow Wow - Salamanca, New York

The Pow Wow was the 10th annual North American Iroquois Veterans Association being held at Veterans Park. This large gathering honors and acknowledges Native American culture and veterans. Yes, Indians are very much proud of their service in the U. S. armed forces.

What was even better than being invited to a Pow Wow was being asked to sit with them on the field instead of in the stands with the spectators. Each tribe/nation was in their own group, and there was Rick and I sitting with them. Our adopted family was Oneida Indians.

Pow Wow
Salamanca, New York

At first, I thought poor Rick really sticks out. When I get tan, I get tan, and with my dark hair, I can blend in, but poor Rick, he looks like a pale face. I felt sorry for him until it was our turn to get up and circle the track with our adoptive family for their native dance.

Each nation took a turn circling the track with a particular dance. The dances can have many meanings. Some are what they call honor dances. These dances honor someone's special occasion, such as birthdays, anniversaries, the loss of a loved one, or other honorable events. Most of the time, a drum is included in the ritual dance. When the family dances around once, the rest of the family and friends join in.

Pow Wow - Salamanca, New York

When it was time for our adoptive family to do their tribute dance, they insisted we get up and join them. Suddenly I felt sorry for myself because I just could not get my feet to go with their beat. Rick jumped right in and never missed a step. He looked like he was one of them. Now I was the one looking like a silly pale face. Oh my!

Thank you, Leta and the Oneida Nation, for making me part of your family. I will never forget how special you made me feel.

One more note, sometimes I assume the wrong thing. There was a black man dressed up in his native dress. So I approached him and said, "Ah, you but be a Blackfoot!" Nope, he wasn't. I won't ask that question again.

Taken off the web:

Oneida Indians, along with the Mohawk, Seneca, Cayuga and Onondaga comprised the original Five Nations of the Iroquois Confederacy that dates back to the 1500s, which later became the Six Nations when the Tuscarora joined in the 1700s.

Tia Smith, Miss Indian World 2002
Salamanca, New York

Chapter Fourteen

Rally Time and the Vanishing Go-Go Bus
Another Epic Adventure
In its Entirety
Grab a Drink – Make a Snack

I try to keep politics out of my travel books, but in this adventure it is a large part of the story. It will give you a glimpse of what goes into a presidential rally. So let's rewind the clock back to 2004, a time when I was actively engaged in the Republican Party and campaigning for President George W. Bush. A time when I thought GOP stood for God's Own Party. A time before I was enlightened.

How did I ever get so involved with politics? I was always politically inclined and always kept a pulse on world affairs ever since I was a child when my family would shout and argue about such matters into the wee hours of the night. But how I got really plugged in was because of Jeff Marshaus, who invited me to a Republican meeting. I said, sure, why not? I will attend. I never knew it was so easy to get involved. From there, it then became sort of a personal challenge to see how far I could go in politics.

I became so active it almost spawned another career when I jumped ship and became Lake County Chairman for the Constitution Party of Ohio. But that's another story! I drifted too far to the right and need to get back on the road and write about the vanishing Go-Go Bus, which is what this story is all about and not my almost political career besides, I shouldn't keep you in suspense any longer, so grab a cup of chair and sit back in your coffee, and I will tell you.

The Set Up – Sounds Like a Sting But It Isn't

Let's begin with the week that led to that very scary and eventful Saturday on Labor Day weekend 2004. It all started on the previous Tuesday when I received a phone call from the Republican Party asking if I could volunteer for President Bush's Lake County appearance on Saturday. Without hesitation, I said yes, even though Kristine had already invited me to her part of Ohio for the entire Labor Day weekend. She had quite a bit planned for us. I figured she would understand. Unfortunately, she didn't. Not until I explained that this is for The President, the most important man in the world, surely you can understand my being late because of the president. After we got that ironed out, all was fine.

Thursday

The committee to reelect W met with the volunteers to discuss details at Meximillians Restaurant (now defunct), which was having another Bush Rally. This mini-rally just warmed us up for the big event on Saturday. The Republican Convention was blaring on their large screen TVs. Coupled that with the buzz and talk surrounding the president's scheduled appearance in two days, made the atmosphere lively and upbeat.

How President Bush spoke at the convention energized the crowd further. His speech made me proud to be an American. My sister Cynthia, who can be very silly, spied a large bag of balloons that were for celebrating after the president was finished speaking. But of course, she couldn't leave the balloons alone. One at a time, she tossed them into the crowd. Throughout the president's speech, people were playing volleyball, hitting them back and forth.

When it ended, we received the necessary information required to volunteer for Saturday's gala. After handshakes and shouts of see you Saturday, we left.

Friday the Day Before the Bus Vanishes
I Get a Ticket

Running late, as usual, I rushed to Representative Steven LaTourette's office in Mentor to pick up the tickets for President Bush's appearance on Saturday. The parking lot was jammed, but I didn't have to wait in line because I was a volunteer. I quickly filled out the necessary paperwork, and once completed, was handed the tickets. Now I know how the boy in Willy Wonka must have felt. On the way out, I briefly spoke with Congressman LaTourette then walked through the crowd clutching my prize.

I went from LaTourette's office directly to Lake Farmpark in Kirtland, where the president was to make his speech. The atmosphere was electric, and the number of people who volunteered to organize was incredible and amazingly diversified. In attendance were men, women, young, old, teachers, firemen, students, teenagers, let's just say from all walks of life. It was equally as exciting to see behind the scenes. The rally was being staged like a mini rock concert. Now I understand where some of my donations go, and yes, both parties do this.

There were two huge semis filled with all sorts of gear. Speakers, platform, fence, the whole show was rolled out from these trucks. As the volunteers listened to their job description, kids painted signs while the Bush roadies sawed, hammered, and hung up all the equipment. The energy and enthusiasm were overwhelming and contagious—everyone who was there pitched in some way. Even people with canes and crutches were handed a responsibility.

The jobs I was offered were escorting and watching the media or crowd control. I decided on crowd control. The description was to make sure no heckler or protester got out of hand. If they did, I was to jump in front of them until the Secret Service took over. The added benefit of this duty was the freedom to roam wherever I wanted.

We worked until about 10:00 p.m. , either making signs or going through our duties and checkpoints. Before leaving, they had four VIP tickets to give away to the person who could guess the birthday of one of coordinators, which luckily I did. I gave those tickets to my folks, who were more than eager to attend the rally.

The Night Before

Went to bed early, but it was impossible to sleep. With all that was planned for Saturday, my mind and body wouldn't relax. Right after the President's rally, I was to leave for Southern Ohio and visit Kristine.

The Morning of the Rally
Less Than 20 Hours Before the Bus Vanishes

About 5:00 a.m. , jumped out of bed and said the heck with trying to sleep, had to be in Kirtland shortly anyway. We were told to be on time because they would take volunteers on a first-come basis. There was a chance more than were needed would show up. That's how great the response was.

It was 6:30 a.m. , the roads to Lake Farmparks were already getting jammed. But I arrived on time for once and had no trouble getting in. The incredibly beautiful sunrise foretold that indeed it would be a special day.

Time was now about 7:00 a.m. Each volunteer group assembled with their leader for final details before going through the security gate. President Bush wasn't to appear until 12:30 p.m. , but the crowd had started gathering.

The OK was given, and the gates were opened. In single file, the volunteers entered, first through the metal detectors and then past the security guards for another check. Once the volunteers were cleared, they sprinted to their designated area. The night before, it was too dark, so you couldn't see how the field was transformed into a stadium. It was exciting banners, ribbons, signs and flags, the media tent, the stage, and the podium where President Bush would stand and give his speech.

After the volunteers were in position, the spectators were allowed to enter – what a mad rush! Since my job description was crowd control, I walked around making sure that no one looked suspicious. One tip they gave us was to look for someone with more clothes on than normal because, underneath, they could be hiding a banner or a derogatory t-shirt or something along those lines.

One of the head volunteers came to where another volunteer and I were standing and yelled, there are flags and signs to pass out. I just grabbed the bull by the horns and put myself in charge. I was swarmed. People were yelling at me from all directions, I need flags, more pompoms for the kids, where are the veterans for Bush signs, sportsmen for Bush, please hurry, bumper stickers, firemen for Bush. There must have been eight boxes of this stuff, I was the only one tossing it out.

Being a volunteer, I could have positioned myself anywhere as long as I kept alert if something needed to be done. Some took advantage of this and stood close to where the president was going to enter or directly in front of the podium, shirking some of their responsibilities. I later regretted this because I lost my spot up close but was able to roam around, help out, talk to people, and keep my promise of doing my job.

Waiting Time

It was now just about impossible to move because of the number of people. The final tally was about 20,000, which was way above the estimate they had figured.

Standing there waiting, I ate a candy bar. When finished, the wrapper was tossed on the ground; there was just no way to get through the mass to find a trash can. An older guy beside me yelled, "What are you doing? Pick it up, don't throw that in front of me." He then told the guy next to him, "Must be a Kerry supporter." He was relentless and kept getting louder. "Pick it up!" I realized that to him, seeing the president was a great honor, and throwing trash on the ground was an insult, but I wasn't the only one. When he yelled, "Are you a Kerry lover?" I had enough. Fearful he might incite the crowd to burn me at the stake, I whispered in his ear, "If you don't shut up, I will have you removed." He did, and I got away from that guy. Being patriotic is one thing, but that was overboard.

No Carey or Kerry

Equally as bad was how my dad felt. He tried getting my attention and hollered "Carey" No reply, so he yelled "Carey louder." People around him gave him dirty looks. That's when he realized they thought he was saying Kerry as in John Kerry. So after that, he called me by my middle name Kevin. And now you know my middle name.

One Hour To Go For the President's Arrival
14 Hours Remaining Before the Bus Vanishes

The country band that was playing stopped and gave way to the speakers, but first an opening prayer, then the pledge of allegiance. Everything was so positive it made you feel good to be alive and American. It is much different than all the negatives the media and the Democratic Party give President Bush and the Republicans. Unless you are at an event like this, you just don't know what you are missing. Among the speakers was Congressman Steven LaTourette, running for reelection and Tim Grendell, running for Ohio Senate. Both speeches drew loud applause from the crowd.

The clouds moved in and it started to drizzle, but that didn't dampen the crowd's enthusiasm the least bit. It was now shoulder to shoulder and impossible to move. Helicopters appeared overhead and circled, which signaled that the president was close by.

Finally, the moment we all waited for some seven hours, "Ladies and gentlemen… the President of the United States"! The noise from the crowd was deafening. Another one of my duties was to play cheerleader, which was definitively not needed to get this crowd yelling.

The president has been doing this for a while, but the look on his face was one of surprise. His expression seemed to say all this for me? It was genuine, nothing fake, shirt sleeves rolled up, just one of us. I was only about 15 feet from him. This is the closest I have ever been to the president, the free world leader, the most important man of the greatest nation. It made me tear up. It was so awesome.

President Bush first spoke about his family and his wife Laura, then about his accomplishments, and concluded with the situation with the terrorists. Throughout his speech, it rained, but he didn't flinch once. He seemed oblivious to it. Not one bad word was spoken from the crowd, nothing but cheers and applause. At 1:30 p.m. President Bush concluded his speech. The crowd, however, was held back until he was safely away.

President Bush
Lake Farmpark - Kirtland, Ohio

The grounds were trampled on, and litter was everywhere. I told someone it looked like a Republican Woodstock. I guess the candy wrapper I dropped was not a big deal after all.

On my way out, I spotted Leon Bibb, a local Cleveland celebrity newscaster. Of course, I had to talk to him. We snapped a few photos together, then I hurried off to the Go-Go Bus just to sit in traffic for another 1 1/2 hours.

It was now off to visit Kristine. The fun had only just begun.

9 Hours to the Disappearance of The Go-Go Bus

It was around 4:00 p.m. when I hit the road to head to Kristine's house in Southern Ohio. Even though I was so ragged from no sleep and not eating, I didn't want to stop for either. I promised Kristine, that I would arrive at 6:00 p.m. , which was not going to happen. It might be possible in my other vehicles but not in the Bus.

The trip down there was uneventful, but interesting. Usually, people give the thumbs up, wave, or act silly when they see the Go-Go Bus. Not this time. It was split between people smiling and waving and people trying not to smile or giving dirty looks. Wonder if it had to do with the large Bush signs on it.

On Rt. 23 south of Columbus, a mini pickup passed me and waved a Kerry bumper sticker out his window. Of course, I couldn't let things be, so I passed him and waved my Bush bumper sticker. This exchange happened a few more times back and forth until I managed to prop a yard sign against the front passenger window. I rode alongside that truck quite a distance with that sign staring at him. I had enough playing, gunned the Bus, and took off.

I made it to Waverly about 7:00 p.m. , not bad timing at all. Stopped at a gas station to refuel and call Kristine. While I was on the phone, someone was blowing their horn as they drove by the gas station. Guess who it was? It was my buddy in the mini pickup still waving that Kerry bumper sticker. How funny.

I told Kristine where I was. She said, don't move, I'll be right there. I realized I was at Noel's Pee Pee Gas. I was here years ago driving through town on the way to Gallipolis with Gary and Seth. How can you forget a place that sells Pee Pee gas? And later on in this story, you will find another reason I will never forget this gas mart. Why do they call it Pee Pee gas? I'll let you find out for yourself. Just ask a local.

As I was filling my tank, Kristine pulls in. We hugged each other, and then bickered – before we do anything, I want to shower and change clothes. No, we won't have time. You don't need a shower. Yes I do. No you don't. I have to change clothes. No you don't. It's a party by the lake, and no one is dressed up. Yes I do. No you don't. Give me directions, and I'll catch up with you. You'll get lost. No I won't. Yes, you will. How about me following you in the Bus to your house so I can park it there? The Bus is too slow, and we won't have time.

Eventually, we decided to park the Bus at the nursing home where Kristine mom works that is directly behind the gas station. Oh boy, was that a wrong decision, hmm, or maybe it was the right decision.

Party Time

We rushed to her place so I could freshen up and change clothes. Jumped into her truck and took off to the party at the lake. Driving to her friend's, the place she said I would never find, it occurred to me that I was also at this lake years prior. The cottage was further down, but I was still there.

The setup was slightly different from what Kristine described, at least in my mind, but her friends were as welcoming as she said. She did warn me though, they are Democrats and take their politics seriously, don't argue with them. They will throw you in the lake. Gee, that is serious!

I had a great time conversing with everyone. One fascinating conversation was with Mike, who played football for Ohio State back in the '70s. It's not as glamorous as it's made out to be.

Because I complained that I didn't eat dinner yet, Kristine reluctantly let me use her truck to go back into town. She was hesitant because she thought I would get lost coming back. While I was out trying to find food, they placed bets whether or not I would get lost. It took longer than expected because I couldn't find a place to eat, but I made it back without incident. I never did find out what the wager was and who won.

After my meal, Kristine wanted me to get in this little plastic paddle boat with her. I kept telling her no way, but she kept insisting I join her. Reluctantly I said OK, but only if you give me a life jacket. We asked Kristine's friend Chuck who was quite happy at this time from drinking for help finding one. He replied, oh, you don't need it. Two little kids chimed in and said the same thing.

Usually, I would never get in a boat of any sort, especially one that dinky and endorsed by kids or someone inebriated. Don't know if I am getting braver or dumber, but they eventually coaxed me in without a life preserver. It was a fun but scary ride. The best part was I didn't drown and die.

The Disappearance

Close to midnight, Kristine and I said goodbye to everyone and left. Reviewing all the events of the day and laughing, that is, until we pulled into the nursing home to retrieve the Go-Go Bus. Suddenly both of us got silent.

Kristine said, "Carey, where's the Bus?" I thought she was joking, but as soon as I got my bearings straight, I realized she wasn't; this was the right parking lot. It was as if I was in the twilight zone. Things got fuzzy. "KRISTINE, IT'S IT'S NOT HERE!" The Go-Go Bus had vanished.

She said the worst thing possible to say when someone is about to have a panic attack and nervous breakdown – "Don't worry! We will find it." Don't worry, I immediately knew then to worry! There we were, as befuddled as you are reading this, as to what happened.

Send in the Cavalry

Immediately I wanted to call the police and report it, but Kristine wanted to wait and think it over. We drove to the exact spot where the Bus was parked, which was the last row of the lot and where her mom parks. There were no crop circles to indicate it was taken by a UFO. But there were tire tracks that led halfway into the grass of the adjacent building's backyard and then stopped. Nothing was adding up.

Between our arguing about what to do and Kristine's trying to calm me down, my mind was going a million miles a minute with what just happened – It's the large Bush signs, this is Democrat country, I parked in a handicapped space, a bunch of rednecks took it, it's out in some field painted John Deere green and used as a hunting lodge, good ole boys are using it for target practice – on and on my mind raced.

Nervously we entered the nursing home to inquire if they saw anything. Yep, they sure did. It was towed a little after I left it. So, that solved one mystery, it was towed, but why? Again my mind raced. It was organized crime, my Bus was in a chop shop, and the parts were being placed on eBay to be sold to members of the A100 van club that I belong to.

Kristine calls the police, only to be told they were out on a call and it will be at least 35 minutes before they could arrive. She then decides to call her mom and vent. "Mom, Carey had the Go-Go Bus towed. Can you believe they would tow his show vehicle? Why would they tow it from this lot unless someone from the nursing home called?"

Mom was clueless and had no idea why they would go into the lot unless someone from the nursing home called. So off we marched back into the assisted living center, only to be told, nope, no one here called, unless it was the shift before us. Hmm, they were giving us the good ole run-around.

Next, Kristine started calling all the tow trucks in the area. She knows most of the drivers in town and thought they would tell her where it was. Nope, not one of the service garages had seen the Go-Go Bus or had any clue to its whereabouts.

While I was pacing like an expectant father waiting for the police to arrive, Kristine gets another brainstorm, "I am going to call the mayor." What person would call the mayor, especially at 1:00 a.m. , to complain about a missing vehicle? Still thinking Kristine was only joking, she surprised me by calling the operator for the mayor's number. Still not believing her, she certainly does indeed call.

Poor guy, all he was able to say was hello, and then it was all Kristine. "Mayor Spencer, this is Kristine of Jackson, my friend from out of town had his show vehicle towed; I want to know why! None of the yards have it, the police station knows nothing, and they said it would be a while before they get here…" on and on, she let it fly.

The mayor wasn't able to get in one word. Abruptly the conversation ended. Beaming with a big smile, Kristine said, "See, I told you, I know what I am doing. He's calling the police station right now and will have them here shortly." I guess living in a small town does have its advantages. I couldn't even get an appointment to set an appointment to speak to my mayor by appointment in the daytime.

I just couldn't take anymore, so I excused myself to use the restroom in the old folk's home. Where's a bottle of Boone's Farm wine when it's needed most?

The Arrival of the Men in Blue

I wasn't gone long, and as I walked out, Kristine was talking to the police. Wow, she wasn't kidding when she said they would be here shortly.

Walking towards them, I see Kristine laughing and having a good ole time with the cops. They were gabbing away and joking as if it was all a prank. How could she act this way? I am in the middle of a nervous breakdown, but it was suddenly all a game to her.

Kristine shouts to me in her southern drawl, "Did yaa pay for the gaaaas?" What the heck is she squawking about gas? I was so stressed from everything I foolishly thought I ran out of gas, and that's why they towed it. But, duh, of course not, how stupid, I drove it into the lot. It just didn't make any sense what she was asking.

I join them and size up the situation. Kristine is smiling. One cop stood a few steps behind his partner. He was the typical policeman, serious, uniform buttoned up and neat. The other reminded me of Andy Taylor of Mayberry, not because of his looks, but because of his mannerisms. The first few buttons of his shirt were undone, and he had a down to earth pleasant demeanor. Like Andy, it seemed as if he didn't need a gun; he could diffuse a situation with his wit and charm.

The head patrolman, the one who reminded me of Andy, spoke up and said, "That's a real nice Buus ya have, we haaaated to tooow it. But did you pay fer your gaaas?" Huh? My gas, why do they keep asking about paying for my gas. Kristine speaks up, "At the station, did ya pay fer it when ya filled uuup?" Oh my goodness. My color went from looking like an anemic ghost to a red tomato with a sunburn. The gas! I completely forgot to pay for my gas!

A Solved Mystery

During the hoopla at the gas station with seeing Kristine and bickering, not to mention no sleep, I pulled out of the gas station without paying. Oh my, what a lamebrain, I completely forgot. We woke up her mom, the mayor, accused everyone, and all this time, it was because I didn't pay for the gas.

Stammering away and trying to explain the situation, my every other word was sorry. The head patrolman interrupted and said in a slow southern drawl, "Oh that's OK, I understand, we haaated to do it because it is a nice buuus. We waaas real caaaareful with it. The tow truck driver was extraaa cautious. He made sure he didn't scratch it."

Possible penalties for a "pump and run" in Ohio could include a fine, jail time, and license suspension, so I was horrified. I must have apologized a dozen more times and felt like such a buffoon, I couldn't even look at Kristine.

The Bus was impounded, but before it could be released, I had to pay for the gas. So the police followed us around the corner to the station to make sure I did.

Kristine wasn't overly concerned with my gaff, so my repeated apologies weren't necessary. She was more irate and upset at the gas mart. All they had to do was walk over and yell at me; instead, they called the police. The nursing home is literally behind the gas mart. But what would you expect from a gas station that sells pee pee gas?

At the counter, I sheepishly paid for the fill-up feeling like a complete idiot with the cop standing next to me to make sure I did. I am still apologizing when he cuts me off and says, "Oh, don't worry, I once drove off in a patrol car without paying."

I am still waiting for the ticket to appear. Instead, the policeman says, "Just follow me to the staaation for the release paaapers." Without question, I jumped back into Kristine's truck. She points out as we were following them, "Did ya notice they haaad two prisoners?" It was weird; they took time out for my stupidity, while they had two people cuffed in the back of their cruiser. From the gas station to the police station, we go.

OK, there you have it, the story of the vanishing Go-Go Bus. Oh, don't tell me you are disappointed, c'mon it was a disappearance, right?

Please Release It Let It Go

Arriving at the Piketon Police Department, Kristine tells me she is so embarrassed. I asked what for? I am the goofball who feels like a complete idiot; what could you be embarrassed about. She replied, "Wait till you see our police station."

And I would have to agree, it was cute and well, um, homey more like a Hillbilly bed and breakfast, very quaint. It reminded me of a suburban ranch-style house converted to a police station. I just love small-town America.

Kristine and I get out of her truck but were told to wait until we were given the OK. They had to bring in their prisoners. One was a disheveled male in cuffs, and the other a waif-looking female, I assume his lover. Besides being dirty and stoned, they seemed harmless. Probably just got carried away in some local bar listening to Lynyrd Skynyrd and arrested for disorderly conduct. Then again, they could have been murderers.

As soon as they were corralled into the holding cell, we were allowed in. I started the apologies all over again, which weren't needed. The release papers were signed, and directions were given to where the Bus was located.

The police were so pleasant that before leaving, formal introductions were made. The one that did all the talking and handled most everything was Corporal Carson. He could have issued a ticket, but realized it was an honest mistake.

Thank you's were given, handshakes exchanged, and excitedly we zoomed off to rescue the missing Go-Go Bus.

It was located outside of town at a place called Heistads towing. Even though I knew where it was and why it was towed, I was still very nervous to see its condition.

The Go-Go Bus Is Freed

As we arrived at the impound, a worker was just pulling in because the place was closed. Usually, a vehicle release would have had to wait until regular business hours, which would have been Monday, but an exception was made. Wonder if the call to the mayor was the reason?

Tim, the tow truck operator, unlocked the door and let us in. I didn't see the Go-Gus Bus and anxiously asked where it was. He reassured us, "Don't worry, it's safe. It's parked in the back of the lot. I was real careful with it and hated to tow it because it's such a nice vehicle." Then he went on to say, "I saw you earlier in the day at a payphone, were you stopped on Rt. 23?" as if there's another purple '69 Xplorer running around. I answered yes, and he replied, "YEP, I sure saw you alright." All this was said, kind of apologetic that the Bus had to be towed but at the same time with pride that he was the one who got the opportunity. I can imagine the talk at the local bar the bragging rights he had – Yeah, but that's nothing. I got to tow the Go-Go Bus – 'nother notch in his belt for sure.

Kristine said she would pay for the charge because she felt as if it was partly her fault. I didn't argue and gladly handed her the bill, which was crazy expensive. It might be small-town America, but the bill was definitely big city.

He took us around back to where the Bus was parked by its lonesome. I explained how worried I was because of the Bush signs all over it, thought for sure it would have been vandalized because it is Democrat country. Kristine speaks up and says "Gawt that right." Tim corrected her and said, "Not really, I'm a Republican, and so are quite a few around here. There's a lot of gun owners who won't vote Democrat."

He handed me the keys. I glanced over the outside of the Bus, and it looked OK, which made me happy. Then I opened the door. One word can accurately describe the mess inside – EARTHQUAKE! It was strewn with all my knickknacks, maps, dishes; everything had rattled loose. Salt and pepper, oregano, and basil were all over. It looked like an episode of Italians Gone Wild. But seriously, have you ever seen that movie The Long Long Trailer with Lucile Ball and Dezi Arnaz? There is a scene in that movie that would help you visualize the chaos inside the Bus.

Not wanting to waste any more time, we decided to drive to Kristine's house and clean the mess in the morning.

Morning Time

We arose from our sleep to face the challenge of cleaning the Go-Go Bus and packing it with goodies for the Labor Day weekend Kristine had planned.

I unraveled her garden hose to fill its water tank, then tossed it aside to grab the food she brought down. (Hint, remember the hose, it will be brought up again.) Kristine wouldn't tell me what she had planned, only to hurry, so I did.

Our Itinerary

Our first stop was a garage sale. Sadly though, it was over, but it worked for the better. Everything that didn't sell was tossed on the tree lawn. So instead of paying for the junk, um used merchandise, we picked the stuff for free. Such a deal!

The next stop was to visit Kristine's friend Mrs. Bernadine Stockmeister. Mrs. Bernadine Stockmeister was very influential in Jackson, Ohio, and the surrounding area building their family fortune from a plumbing business. What a character. She wears a gold necklace with three custom charms. One charm is a drippy faucet with a diamond coming out. Another is a bathtub with a pearl, diamond, and ruby in it. And the third charm I liked best is the tiny toilet with a lid that opens with two diamonds sitting in the bowl for toilet paper.

I was given a tour of Bernadine's house, including the basement, that she calls a shrine to the presidents. She has met every president since President Ford and may have met a few before him. Her favorite was President Ronald Reagan. When I told Bernadine I had volunteered at Lake Farmparks for President Bush's appearance, it made her day. After that, she acted all giddy and asked me repeatedly about what time the President left. Kristine told me the reason for her actions was because she had a secret; I found out later that secret, Bernadine had dinner with President Bush when he made his way through Southern Ohio.

So far, so good, tree lawn shopping, talking politics, now off to Lake Snowdon, not sure for what, but we were off to Lake Snowdon.

Lake, Rattle and Roll

Lake Snowdon is six miles southwest of Athens, Ohio, and is the home of the Pawpaw Festival. What is a pawpaw? If you guess the opposite of a mama, you are wrong. It is North America's largest native tree fruit.

Upon entering the park, a campsite was chosen, then Kristine and I made our way to a roped-off area that had a stage erected. Judging from the age of the mostly female crowd, I thought it was a lecture on how to make quilts. I was a good sport, though, said nothing, and went along with setting up our blanket and cooler.

At 6:00 p.m. sharp, the crowd started cheering as... as... hey, is that Elvis! Oh, MY GOODNESS! I have seen all kinds of Elvis imitators and performers. Fat ones, Chinese ones, but this guy was eerily Elvis reincarnate. He came out in a jacket that Elvis wore in Speedway. I mentioned it to Kristine, and right after I said it, this reborn Elvis said, "Tonight, I am wearing a jacket that Elvis wore in Speedway." If you want to win a southern girl's heart, love Elvis and NASCAR.

Anyway, I was literally in awe over this guy's performance; it was that incredible! Not only his voice but every movement Elvis did, he perfected. Up close, he may not look like Elvis, but we were sitting far enough back where the illusion was complete. Halfway through the show, there was an intermission. When he retook the stage for the next set, he was now the Vegas Elvis.

Wow, I am telling you that you have to see this performer. His name is one you won't forget. It is Dwight Icenhower, yes, almost like our former president.

I asked Kristine why is talent this good is being wasted on a small crowd at a campground. She explained that Dwight is very humble, and even though he does major shows, it hasn't gone to his head. This particular show was a fundraiser for Carbondale Community Center.

Dwight played until sundown, but the audience wasn't about to go away. To keep him singing, a lady jumped up and held a flashlight on him. After a few encores, the show finally ended because of darkness.

Dwight made his way to a table to sign autographs and sell his CDs. Somehow I had to meet him, but how, I wasn't about to stand in line behind 50 giggling middle-aged women.

Just then, while watching Dwight's fans hold lighters and flashlights over him, I got a brainstorm! I ran off to the Go-Go Bus and started her up. Kristine thought I was leaving, not at all. I pulled the Bus directly in front of his table, put on my high beams, grabbed my spotlight, and lit up the whole area.

Dwight took notice, and with that, I grabbed the opportunity to introduce myself. He excused himself for a few minutes to meet me and to look at the Bus. Kristine took a few photos of Dwight sitting in it and one next to me.

After a performance like that, I made sure he received an official "Cruising Across America Go-Go Bus t-shirt." (I might as well plug my merchandise). As we were leaving, I heard him yell "Carey, I got your t-shirt on".

What a performance! It had me all hyped up.

How could this weekend be any better, president, politics, garbage picking, and Elvis, what's next? Hold on, we are getting there.

Dwight Icenhower inside the Go Go Bus
Lake Snowdon, Ohio

From Lake to River We Go

We are almost nearing the conclusion of this epic adventure so hold on.

From Lake Snowdon to an Ohio River boat cruise to a river island. Kristine's Uncle Ray Swick, the curator for Blennerhassett Museum and Blennerhassett Island Historical State Park, gave Kristine guest passes to the museum and the island tour. This is another must-see.

The trip to Blennerhassett Island starts off from Point Park in Parkersburg, West Virginia. That is where you board the Island Belle, a 19th century-style sternwheeler. The scenic ride is about 20 minutes to the island. During the cruise to the island, the captain allowed Kristine to grab the wheel and navigate the boat.

Tours of Blennerhassett Island offers a glimpse of what life would be like on a colonial plantation. The volunteers wear period costumes and conduct tours. Self-guided walking tours and horse-drawn wagon rides also are available. Kristine was a bit upset that I was cheap, um frugal, and decided to save the $5. 00 wagon ride fee, so instead, we walked behind the wagon and followed it.

I just loved this part of the trip: laid back, no hurry, very scenic. Thank you Ray Swick, for the passes.

And Now the End Is Near

After all that adventurous fun and laughs and mayhem, you would think the ending would go something like this: and they lived happily ever after – um not exactly. So how did this fantastic odyssey end?

A short distance from Kristine's house my stomach erupted, and that's what it felt like. Going nonstop for five days straight and not eating right, I got the worse stomachache, indigestion, cramps, and whatever other ailment that goes with gastralgia.

Maybe it was the last place we got carry-out. I don't remember what I ordered, but I know Kristine ordered chicken livers. Maybe it was watching her eat the chicken livers that triggered my episode. I doubt it but you never know.

I barely made it back to Kristine's. I zoomed into her drive, turned off the Bus, ran to the back and plopped on the bed, laid flat on my back. But nope, I couldn't be left in peace to die. Kristine starts shouting "Carey, what is all that water? And there is water coming from the garage." "Not now, Kristine I am dying, I don't care if it's a monsoon coming from your garage." "What is this water, what did you do!" "Kristine please, I am not well, no please, no, I can't talk." And then a stern lecture from Kristine followed or maybe more like a tongue lashing, yeah it was a tongue lashing. "Well do you remember during the Woodward Dream Cruise and you didn't pull over when I was sick. Well do you?" There is no worse feeling than being so sick that you think you are dying while being yelled, at and you can't say a darn thing because you're too miserable and you know the person is right. You just lay there hoping the end is near.

So what was all that water? Do you remember the garden hose I used to fill the Go-Go Bus's water tank that I tossed aside to grab the food Kristine brought down? Whew that was a long sentence. The nozzle on the hose broke and water ran from whenever it erupted until we arrived home.

What about the water coming from the garage? Her freezer broke.

So that's how this trip ended? No but that's how I will conclude this story.

Chapter Fifteen

Labor Day Weekend
Africans, Buddnark 'n More

It's been a learning process that has taken me years to learn that if something goes wrong, that's my luck. Um, yes, but that's not what I wanted to write, though. If something goes wrong, just go with the flow and see what comes up or where you're led, and most of the time, things will turn out OK, as in this case.

I was planning on attending «The Glenn Christian Ox Roast Car Show» on Labor Day. I wanted to enter the Go-Go Bus. It sorely lacked sparkle from just sitting. So I worked in earnest all week like a crazed squirrel to bring it up to show condition. And then it happened.

Now don't laugh because this is the truth. A magnet got stuck on the Go-Go Bus. I know what you're thinking… well, that's what a magnet should do, but not like this. I mean, it got stuck. It cost me a set of finger-nails and a chip in the paint to remove it. It was Mom who came to the rescue and suggested a wooden popsicle stick. If not, I may still be out there. In the end, that stupid magnet cost me over an hour and a half.

So you are probably asking yourself, why didn't I just leave the magnet alone. Well, it was a fairly large American flag magnet, and when I went to remove it to wax underneath, it broke, and only half came off. How could anyone show a vehicle with half a US flag and half a US flag that was crooked? It had to come off.

About that lost hour and a half…

The deadline for the car show registration was 7:00 p.m. Friday. I am approximately one hour and thirty minutes away. I start to pull out of my drive at 6:20 p.m. when reality hits me. Even though it is the Go-Go Bus, it really is the go-slow bus. I never would have made it not, in the Bus and not even in a rocket ship, so I pulled back in and parked. It was that darn magnet that upset all of my plans. Friday was a bust, but the rest of the weekend turned out just fine, all because of that magnet. So it was on to plans B, C, and D.

Julia, my Kenyan friend, invited me the day before to an east African gathering in the park, and Walt called to remind me of his 30th school reunion that he wanted me to attend with him.

A huge car show with free food and free everything in exchange for an African outing and a school reunion for a school I didn't attend, all because of a magnet. Did I mention the magnet already? What a tradeoff. Don't laugh, this is real; but now I am glad the magnet got stuck, but Gary Buddnark, I'm not sure. Who's that? I'll get to him.

This is the email Julia sent me:

Please join The Ohio Association of East Africans (TOAFEA) for a fully charged afternoon of fun events and tantalizing food at North Chagrin Reservation. We will be at the Strawberry picnic area. Let's get together to celebrate with refreshments, great food, good friends and a goat barbeque. Pass the message along to all your friends from the East African Community.

I told my friends where I was going on Saturday and said I will just tell Julia's group I am the white sheep of the family. I thought it may be awkward, but I'm glad I went. It turned out to be a fantastic time. It gave me a glimpse of what it is like for foreigners to come to America and some of the hardships they face in settling and getting acclimated.

The organizer of the event gave a short speech about what the group was all about. The one thing that stood out was when he said we are gathered here for many reasons, and one reason is if you need to be bailed out of jail, we are even here for that. He went on to explain when someone asked him exactly what he meant. This is for if you have a bad day and run a red light or something like that but not for criminal activity. I wondered if all foreigners face this or just Africans or all people of color?

The food they served was wonderful. I won't even try to tell you what I ate because I don't know. All I remember was the goat and some kind of beef and spinach dish. Everything was delicious. There are only so many foods. Most nationalities eat the same thing, but it's how the food is prepared and what seasonings are used that differentiates it. I enjoyed what I ate and had a fun time conversing and learning new things about their culture.

I asked the lady at our table what part of Africa she was from. She looked at me strangely and almost angry and said, "I AM AN AMERICAN, do I look like an African?" Uh – how do you answer that? So I thought quickly and said, "Sometimes I assume the wrong thing." NEXT question, please.

Before leaving, I told Julia I brought the Go-Go Bus and invited her for a quick ride. Walking towards the parking lot, I asked her to see if she can find the purple Bus. She replied I think I can see it. Well, I sure hope so. Julia and her friend climbed in, and I drove them around the duck pond and back. After the short cruise, instead of leaving them at the parking lot, I went right up to the shelter where everyone was gathered. Before I could even open the door, there was a rush.

What is this thing? One kid asked do you sell ice cream. Another remarked, wow, this is a house on wheels. So it was another trip around the park, and the count this time was seven on board.

I had an ideal spot in mind to show them – Squire's Castle. Everyone thought I was just joking. They didn't think there was an actual castle in the park. Well, they were very much surprised when they saw it. The timing was just perfect when we arrived. Squire's Castle sits atop a hill; it was a little after dusk, just enough light and circling over it were bats. Seriously!

We had a great time walking around the castle and just acting silly there and then driving back to the picnic.

I dropped them off, but felt terrible because another group wanted a ride. Oh well had to leave. It was time to meet Walt.

I met up with Walt at his reunion. Everyone Walt talked to he would introduce me this way, "This is Carey, my wife couldn't make it, so he is my date." I quickly had enough of that real fast, so I went over to the table where people signed in, and lo and behold, just what I was looking for, a name tag, Gary Buddnark, this one should work.

I slapped it on my chest and rejoined Walt. "Hey Gary, I remember you. You use to wrestle." "I did? I was into science." "Oh, come on, you wrestled." "Well, one time, I wrestled the teacher." "Are you guys trippin'? You drunk? You were pretty good at wrestling." "I'm sorry I had brain damage and don't remember much, maybe I did wrestle."

Another lady thought I was sick because she remembered Gary as being taller and heavier. And then she blurted out, "OH, YOU ARE NOT GARY BUDDNARK!" "Yes, I am." "You know why I know? Because that's his best friend right there, and he just told me."

I walked over to the guy she just pointed at who was laughing at me. I said, "Hey, best friend, so glad to meet you." They showed me Gary's photo in the yearbook and remarked, you know, I guess you could sort of pass for him. After some small talk and info on Gary, I pieced it together and ran with it.

When the next person came up to me, I had my routine all ready. Hi, remember me? I use to wrestle – my brothers did too – I was sick, that's why I am thinner. It was a riot. The best reaction was from a lady Walt introduced me to earlier in the night before I wore the name tag. She saw us again and said hi to Walt once more, and noticed my name tag. "Gary Buddnark??? Now I am confused. You are Gary?" "Yes, I am Gary." "Huh? Was your brother here?" "Yep, and he looks exactly like me." "OK, now that makes sense."

I even posed for a few photos for their school reunion with the name tag on. I wonder if it will make their booklet.

About an hour later, the lady sitting with Gary's best friend ran up to me and said, "Give me the name tag. The real Gary is here." "OUCH! I think it's time to go." "No, come here so you can meet him." When Gary saw me, he made a fist like he wanted to knock me out as someone tipped him off that an imposter was masquerading around as him. But my wit beat him to the punch. I hope I did you well, I did my best. I told everyone I was an excellent wrestler. He eventually calmed down. They even took our photo together. Before I left, I walked over to Gary's best friend and said, "I feel sad. I feel like I just lost my best friend."

Hey, memories were made. Who knows, at the next reunion, maybe I will get an invite or fill in for Gary if he can't attend. At least they will have something else to talk about... remember the two Gary's at our last reunion.

Sunday was another OK, fun day. I forgot I won tickets to the Irish Festival at the Lake County Fairgrounds, all this culture, African, Irish, Buddnark, whatever culture that is. I had two tickets but went by myself. As I was parking, a man was just getting out of a car next to me with out-of-town plates. He saw the Bus and said "Wow that is cool"! I asked if he wanted a ticket, he said sure. They drove up from Columbus about 150 miles away to attend what they thought was the Oktoberfest. As I walked away, they were still squabbling about it. Later on, I found out the Oktoberfest was at the Berea Fairgrounds, about 45 miles from the Lake County Fairgrounds. German Octoberfest – Irish festival, what's the difference, both have beer, besides at least they now had one free ticket.

These cultural fests are turning into really bland, generic events or simply American. I thought I stuck out amongst the pale face, but not as much as the ladies manning the coffee and snack booth where I bought coffee from. The lady asked, "Do you want SHOEGAR?" "Aww, you must be Filipino." "Yes, I am." For those that don't know, shoegar is sugar in Filipino-ese.

But what is weirder than an Italian American buying coffee from a Filipino at an Irish fest? A Hawaiian doing his native dance. What happened to the Irish stepdance? All I could think of was the Irishman who set up the entertainment for this Irish festival had to be drunk.

I didn't stay long, with this sort of entertainment who would, besides my sister and niece, were waiting for me to go to Geneva on the Lake, more culture, biker's culture.

The last official summer vacation weekend and GOL was not nearly as busy as it usually is. I managed to park the Bus right on the strip, which rarely happens. And you know what followed, right? Well, if you have been on any of my adventures or traveled along by reading my books, then you know.

Can I look inside? What is this?

I have had this vehicle for many years, and it is still turning heads and making people gawk.

My sister Cindi, my niece Tiffany, and I walked the entire strip. After our stroll, we bought fries and sat inside the Bus to eat our snack. And yes, a whole new crowd came and went.

One man stepped in and wouldn't leave. I love purple, I love old Dodges, man is this neat, I mean I love this, I really do, man is this cool. His sons tried prying him away, but he wanted to stay. They took off, and about 10 minutes later, he finally left to find them.

Since my teen years, it's been a tradition of mine to visit GOL at least twice a summer. My parents took the family, and the excitement of seeing it as a child never left. It's not a complete summer if I don't visit. So it was a perfect ending to an eventful weekend and an excellent way to end the vacation season: Goodnight, Geneva on the Lake. See you next year.

Oh, wait, one more day to go, Monday, Labor Day. How could I forget? Rich left a message midweek about taking a day drive. The plan he came up with was a drive on Rt. 6 to Andover, into Linesville, Pennsylvania, "Where the Ducks Walk on the Fish", to feed the fish, go to Corry to visit our mutual friend Dennis, and then end the day in Waldemeer Family Amusement Park in Erie.

So what happened? We drove Rt. 6 to Andover, into Linesville, Pennsylvania, "Where the Ducks Walk on the Fish", fed the fish, went to Corry and visited our mutual friend Dennis, and then ended the day in Waldemeer Family Amusement Park in Erie. All went just as Rich had planned.

Some trivia for you. Waldameer is German and means "woods by the sea," which is where Waldemeer Family Amusement Park is located – by the lake.

This is terrible, just terrible. I paid over $100 that is nonrefundable to one of those ancestry websites to find out my genealogy. The reply I got back was: "We could not help you, no one will admit being related to you, sorry, please try again in the near future."
Just terrible.

Chapter Sixteen

Making the Rounds

It's hard to hide when driving the Go-Go Bus. For sure, it's not the vehicle to rob a bank or to pick your nose in. Someone is always looking at it, for example as in this story.

I took the Go-Go Bus out for a short spin and stopped at Rounders Lounge in Mentor for lunch. By the way, they make an excellent burger. I walked in, and a lady immediately greeted me.

"Hey, is that YOUR vehicle?" "Ah yes, it is."

"My friend just posted it on Facebook, you're famous well sort of, my friend was driving through Willoughby, here read her message."

She handed me her cell, and there was a picture of the Go-Go Bus at a store I had just visited with the caption of "What the heck is that"?

The lady then ran outside and took a photo of the Bus and replied to her friend with these words: "I have no clue, but there is one in the lot of Rounders; I think they're invading."

I went to an eye doctor and was
so upset. I didn't see the fine print
until after I got my glasses.

Chapter Seventeen

Big Foot and Little Foot

So there I was at Payless Shoes when a lady said, "Excuse me, what do you think of these shoes?" She was an older lady, under 100 but still old.

She went on to explain, "See, I have this problem. My feet are so big I have to wear men's shoes. They fit better."

Not wanting her to feel bad, I opened up to her. "Since you told me that, I will share with you my problem, which is the opposite. My feet are so small, I wear women's socks because with men's socks, the heel ends up in the middle of my leg."

Then it occurred to me as I looked down at her oversized manly feet and looked at my lady-sized tootsies I thought to myself – Oh my goodness, we have transgender feet!

Did I tell you about the artificial tree I have?
This artificial tree is so realistic that this
morning I found an artificial bird sitting in it.

Chapter Eighteen

Last Words

I mentioned Dad in my introduction and his qualities of enjoying life, laughing, and joking. So I thought I should include this short story of Dad's last words.

Dad had a massive stroke a month before his 89th birthday. He almost made his goal of living until 90. The stroke left him speechless and blind, but his right arm had movement.

He kept moving his hand. I got the impression he was trying to communicate with us. So I grabbed a pen and paper, placed the pen in his hand, put his hand with the pen on the paper. I then told Dad to write something for us. And sure enough, he did, in cursive as he always wrote.

What message did Dad write us?

"I am writing something for U"

I said DAD, come on. So I switched pens and put a marker in his hand to make it easier to write. This time his message was, "I wanna be there when when the" Huh? I turned the paper over, and then dad wrote, "I'll be down to get you in a taxi." Those were his last words. What does that mean?

My sister Cynthia said, "Wait, that is an old song, Dean Martin sang it, "Darktown Strutters Ball".

I'll be round to get you in a taxi, honey – Pick you up 'bout half past eight

Seeing this is a book about travel, how appropriate. Well, Dad, when does the taxi arrive for us?

Wow, did that make for some misty-eyed writing!

And Now For the Conclusion of this Book
I Hope You Enjoyed the Ride

Hey Gang,

Life is meant to be lived to its fullest; it is a continuous journey and adventure.

Therefore, this book does not have an ending. There is still plenty of living to do and more stories to tell. So until I see you again or until my next book is released, keep smiling, travel life, and Carey On…

In the meantime, who knows, maybe those of you mentioned in my books will run into each other and ask – what page are you on? And that could start a friendship and a new chapter in your life.

To be continued…

Stay in touch or share your feedback at www. gogobus. cc

Some people have a one track mind.
Not me. I have an eight lane freeway with
several cloverleaf's at rush hour mind.
Maybe that's why I am congested.

Printed in the USA
CPSIA information can be obtained
at www.ICGtesting.com
LVHW021110181123
764310LV00035B/878